Determinants of Level of Sustainability Report

Determinants of Level of Sustainability Report

Clement Lamboi Arthur, Ph.D.

Copyright © 2018 by Clement Lamboi Arthur, Ph.D.

ISBN: Softcover   978-1-5434-8852-4
        eBook   978-1-5434-8853-1

All rights reserved. No part of this book may be reproduced or transmitted in any form or by any means, electronic or mechanical, including photocopying, recording, or by any information storage and retrieval system, without permission in writing from the copyright owner.

Any people depicted in stock imagery provided by Thinkstock are models, and such images are being used for illustrative purposes only. Certain stock imagery © Thinkstock.

Print information available on the last page.

Rev. date: 01/26/2018

To order additional copies of this book, contact:
Xlibris
800-056-3182
www.Xlibrispublishing.co.uk
Orders@Xlibrispublishing.co.uk
772605

Table of Contents

Abstract xi
Acknowledgements xiii

Chapter 1   Concept of corporate social responsibility 1

    1.1 Introduction 1
    1.2 The grounding assumptions 3
    1.3 Evolution of the concept of corporate social responsibility 7
    1.4 CSR policy and practices in Ghana 12
    1.5 Sustainability reporting practices 14
    1.6 Conclusion 17

Chapter 2   Applicable theories of sustainability reporting practices 18

    2.1 Introduction 18
    2.2 Stewardship theory 19
    2.3 Managerial theories 20
    2.4 Decision usefulness theory 21
    2.5 Economic theories 22
    2.6 Accountability theory 23
    2.7 Political economy theory (PET) 26
    2.8 Stakeholder theory 27
    2.9 Legitimacy theory 30
    2.10 Voluntary disclosure theory (VDT) 35
    2.11 The theoretical application and justification 36
    2.12 Conclusion 42

Chapter 3   Sustainability reporting frameworks 44

    3.1 Introduction 44
    3.2 International Standard ISO 26000:2010 (ISO 26000) 45
    3.3 UN Global Compact 46

3.4 Principles for Responsible Investment Initiative (PRI) 46
3.5 Performance Standards of International Finance
     Corporation (IFC) 47
3.6 Policy on Social and Environmental Sustainability 48
3.7 Extractive Industries Transparency Initiative (EITI) 49
3.8 Fundamental Principles for the Mining Sector (Berlin
     Guidelines) 49
3.9 International Organization for Standardization (ISO
     26000 and ISO 14000) 49
3.10 AccountAbility 1000 (AA1000) 50
3.11 Environmental Excellence in Exploration (E3) 50
3.12 ICMM Principles for Sustainable Development 51
3.13 Voluntary Principles on Security and Human Rights 51
3.14 The Global Reporting Initiative Guidelines 51
     3.14.1 Strategy and profile disclosures 55
     3.14.2 Management approach disclosure 55
     3.14.3 Performance Indicators 56
3.15 Conclusion 57

Chapter 4   Content analysis in the sustainability reporting research ... 58

4.1 Introduction 58
4.3 Content analysis procedures 64
4.4 Units of measurement 66
4.5 Validity and reliability 68
4.6 Descriptive statistics 71
4.7 Correlation analysis 73
4.8 Regression analysis 78

   4.8.1 Size of MCG and the level of SR 81
   4.8.2 Growth rates and the level of SR 83
   4.8.3 Profitability ratio and the level of SR 84
   4.8.4 Efficiency ratio and the level of SR 86
   4.8.5 Capital gearing ratio and the level of SR 87
   4.8.6 Working capital and the level of SR 89
   4.8.7 Age of the MCG and the level of SR 90
   4.8.8 Complexity of the MCG and the level of SR 91
4.9 Conclusion 92

Chapter 5   Managerial and Policy Implications 94

    5.1 Introduction 94
    5.2 The main findings and conclusion 94
    5.3 Managerial and policy implications 96
    5.4 Conclusion 97

References 99

List of Tables

Table 1.1 CSR Definitions 9

Table 1.2 Drivers of Corporate Social Responsibility..............................11

Table 3.1 IFC Performance Standard on Environmental and
          Social Sustainability..47

Table 3.2 SR indicators in GRI guidelines 54

Table 4.1 Dependent and Independent Variables 60

Table 4.2 Independent Variables Measurement and Justification 61

Table 4.3 The Coding Units..68

Table 4.4 Descriptive statistics 72

Table 4.5 Correlation matrix between the dependent and
          independent variables..76

Table 4.6 Regression of the characteristics
          determining the level of SR.. 80

Abstract

The aim of the study is to examine the determinants of the level of sustainability reports of mining companies in Ghana in the absence of regulatory and statutory requirements. With the use of content analysis the thesis started by probing the question of whether there is an effect of factors such as size, growth rate, profitability, efficiency, gearing ratio, working capital ratio, age and complexity of the mining companies on the level of disclosure in sustainability report. The study by reviewing some of the traditional theories used in the accounting literature, adopted the legitimacy and stakeholder theories to examine sustainability reporting practices by mining companies in Ghana. While the arguments presented by the proponents of the legitimacy theory is used to explain how these companies may prepare sustainability reports to appear as having the same norms and values as those of the society, the arguments in support of the stakeholder theory are used to explain heterogeneous stakeholders views. The empirical investigation was started after methodological issues that are believed to be relevant to this research project are discussed. The investigation found that there are significant effects of corporate size (positive), gearing, working capital and complexity of MCGs (negative) on the level of SR whilst no significant effects of growth rate, profitability, efficiency and the age of the company on the level of Sustainability Report were found in spite of the increasing level of the report.

Acknowledgements

I would like to thank Almighty God in first place for seeing me through. The completion of this thesis has been the most challenging but desirable activity in my entire life. This doctoral journey has been made possible due to a significant contributions and assistance of many individuals towards this unforgettable experience. First of all, I would like to express my deepest gratitude to Dr Junjie Wu, my Director of Studies, for her supervision, critical remarks, commitment, endless support, encouragement and in particular, for her time and dedication on this work. I also owe many thanks to my supervisor, Dr Milton Yago for reviewing and commenting on my work, his valuable help and important suggestions during the preparation of this thesis. Finally, my greatest gratitude goes to my dearest family Adelaide Arthur, Lydia Danso, Elizabeth Cobbah, Millicent Cobbah, Susana Cobbah, Agnes Cobbah, Anthea Ethel Arthur, Clement Calvin Arthur Jnr., Fiona Evicta Arthur, Luther Micheal Arthur and Lysha Nina Lamboi Arthur for praying and supporting me at all times.

This work is dedicated to my late grandmother
Madam Mary Mensah and Late father Mr Charles Evans Arthur
who left too soon to see me as a doctor.

Chapter 1

Concept of corporate social responsibility

1.1 Introduction

Today businesses have employed sustainable development as one of the main strategy to fulfil the expectation of their stakeholders by reporting how they work with sustainability. In spite of a broad acceptance that we need to work for sustainability there is still debate on how best to define and describe sustainable development. According to Isaksson and Steimle (2009) organisations are monitored by their stakeholders to find an acceptable strategy for requirement of publishing a sustainability report. According to Brundtland Report (1987) definition, sustainable development and sustainability is well quoted and forms a good starting point (Isaksson and Steimle, 2009). "Sustainable development is development that meets the needs of the present generation, without compromising the ability of future generations to meet their own needs" (WCED, 1987). It is also termed as "providing a good life for everybody" and "safeguarding a healthy nature" (Isaksson and Garvare, 2003). Consequent to these definition, the Brundtland Report can be interpreted here with the identification of two main stakeholders namely humanity and nature. Freeman and Reed (1983) defined stakeholder as "Any identifiable group or individual who can affect the achievement of an organization's objectives or who is affected by the achievement of an organization's objectives".

It can be deduced from the definition that the natural environment (animals, plants, natural resources etc.) is also a stakeholder (Starik, 1995). Due to the fact that nature is an indispensable prerequisite for human life and resource relationships between the nature and economy it has been argued that it should be considered as the primordial stakeholder (Stead and Stead, 2000; Driscoll and Starik, 2004; Isaksson and Steimle, 2009). The economic development needed by the humanity to solve their problems should be done in such a way to prevent destruction to the resources needed for the future generations who are also stakeholders. The reliance on humanity and nature means that the role of companies supports sustainability. According to Isaksson and Steimle (2009) even if corporate success is a condition for generating value this should not be at the expense of the core stakeholders. They are of the view that sustainable development is not only an issue for nations but also for companies.

It is considered that success of many companies depends on the relationship of stakeholder groups and on the resources they deliver. The mining companies in Ghana (MCGs) are expected to adopt practices not only to show how they work towards sustainability by reducing pollution, but also their ability to communicate satisfactorily to their stakeholders since they must obtain the social licence to operate (Isaksson and Steimle, 2009). Hence the preparation of sustainability report must be in a form acceptable to all the stakeholders, from market-related stakeholders (customers, shareowners, suppliers) to internal (e.g. employees, board of directors) or societal stakeholders (e.g. government, communities, MIs, NGOs). It is assumed that the variety of the stakeholders and their concerns led to corporate responsibility including economic, environmental and social aspects (Zink and Steimle, 2007). This means that, to act socially responsible means not only abiding by the legal regulations, but also going beyond compliance and investing more into human capital, the environment and the relations with stakeholders (Isaksson and Steimle, 2009). In this Chapter, the grounding assumptions behind the study are reiterated. It also focuses on the narrower part of the literature and concentrates on the review of the existing empirical literature. Evolution of the concept of corporate social responsibility and CSR policy and practices in Ghana, as well as sustainability reporting practices, are presented.

1.2 The grounding assumptions

The global financial crisis which began in 2008 manifested itself in 2009 with negative effects on the performance of the global mining industry as the prices of the bulk of metals witnessed significant depreciation. In an environment of heightened scrutiny, most mining companies continued to contend with the rising costs of regulatory compliance and sustainable development. In spite of the challenges, Ghana's mining sector performed quite creditably in 2009. According to the Ghana Statistical Service and Ministry of Finance and Economic Planning, the mining sub-sector grew at a remarkable rate of 8% as compared with the 5.5% in 2008. By the end of the year 2009, the industry had given a direct employment to a total of 12,294 people; 98% Ghanaians and 2% expatriate (www.ghanachamberofmines.org/site/publications).

Mining in Ghana as in elsewhere do not come without inherent problems to the stakeholders. There is a well-known general negative perception of the mining industry due to the harmful nature of its activities particularly to the environment and the community in general. The existence of illegal mining in Ghana continued on some member companies' concessions over the years has been on the ascendancy. The phenomenon however took an alarming dimension as illegal miners expanded their activities onto public lands and in water bodies polluting and destroying these natural resources extensively. It has been reported that (Daily Graphic, 27th July 2011) the recent flood in the Eastern region of Ghana was as a result of the activities of these illegal miners. Registered companies are also part of these problems. Many mining towns and cities have become dead cities with less economic activities. Farming which have been the main source of livelihood is almost wipe out through the activities of the mining causing a lot of unemployment with it related problems such as arm robbery, prostitution, urban migration, poverty, to mention a few.

A major challenge in this regard is the evolving environmental and social costs of extracting mineral resources; due to its environmental impacts through poor waste management, lack of rehabilitation, and emphasis on production over environmental impacts on mining industry. The environmental and social health of a region and community has been affected by mining positively or negatively remains a contentious area for the sustainability debate and the mining industry (Hancock, 1993), particularly for the developing world (e.g. Ali, 2006; Kumah, 2006). This in turn is closely related to social impacts and challenges of varying degrees of difficulty. Several discussion and debate have been made about how sustainable is the current ways of mining especially in developing countries like Ghana. This brings the question of whether future mining will cost more than at present or the devastation that the activities of mining is causing is really justifiable. Governmental institutions have employed several sanctions including taxes to punish or bring some of the offenders to order but have not been able to achieve the said goals. In Ghana due to the poor financial position of mining institutions (Environmental Protection Agency and Minerals Commission) mandated to check and regulate some of these offenses have crippled such initiatives.

Mining companies are in recent times being pressurised to widen their scope for corporate public accountability by many groups including the governments, Non-Governmental Organisations (NGOs) and other stakeholders have resulted in measuring and reporting on their environmental and social impacts (Lozano and Huisingh, 2011; Lozano, 2013). The current measuring and reporting of the environmental and social impacts have also been considered not adequate; there is the need to adopt the preparation of sustainability reporting which involves the economic element of sustainability as well as integrating the environmental, social and economic performance data and measures.

The main aim of this book is to assess the determinant of the level of sustainability report by the Mining Companies in Ghana (MCGs) in the absence of any regulatory requirements or any recognition by the professional bodies. The type of performance indicators to be disclosed in the SR is very important in the sense that the level of disclosure of information will have a great impact on the decision making ability of the managers as well as the policy makers. Therefore the rationale behind this study is to draw attention, if any, to the current sustainability reporting practices by the mining companies in Ghana with respect to the effect of their characteristics on the level of Sustainability Report (SR) and suggesting recommendations for policy decisions.

Besides, Corporate Social Responsibility (CSR) in general have become the integral part or aspect of business operations to the extent where most organisations have incorporated them into their vision and missions statements as well as value statements the world over (Ofori and Hinson, 2007; Adams, 2004; Archiel, et al., 2008; Gray, et al., 2001). Furthermore, the voluntary nature of the preparation of SR by entities does not mandate MCGs to conform its contents to a particular sustainability framework initiative such as the Global Reporting Initiatives (GRI) for example, hence the content compromised. This makes it very difficult to compare even entities in the same sector. There is the need to prepare the SR in order to meet the regulatory requirements of the country to reduce potential non-compliance cost which has increase over the years. Managers sometimes produce bad information to avoid legal actions taken against the company but such inadequate disclosure or decrease in disclosure may be harmful to the company. Therefore preparation of SR will enable the stakeholders to make a meaningful critique about the activities of the reporting entity in relation to their sustainability practices thereby enabling them to monitor the entity's compliance to the guidelines (Tilt, 2001).

There is a growing interest and commitment regarding sustainability reporting (Leeson and Ivers, 2005) and plays a key role in modern organizations in the provision of public services, for which accountability is essential (Guthrie et al., 2010). Even though transparency requirements and accountability are increasing, reporting on sustainability and social responsibility as a topic has not yet been widely studied (Ball and Grubnic, 2007; Ball and Bebbington, 2008; Navarro et al., 2010). Acording to Lamprinidi and Kubo (2008) the reasons why public agencies' are interested in disclosing their sustainability information are not different from those of private companies. Their reasons included the need to show the effort they are making in relation to climate change and other sustainability issues; growing interest in and demands for transparency and accountability; explanation of management activities to stakeholders; to show their leadership in the sector; and existence of sustainability rankings that seek to promote the release of sustainability reports and share the benefits (Lamprinidi and Kubo, 2008). These reason also motivated the study.

Furthermore, it is an area where little has been done in the emerging economies (Kisenyi and Gray, 1998; Ofori and Hinson, 2007), even though companies are increasingly disclosing CSR information (Gray et al., 2001; Adams, 2004; Archel et al., 2008). Whilst most of these studies are done in the developed countries (Adams, 2002; O'Dwyer et al., 2002; 2005; Lamberton, 2005; Gray, 2010; Smith et al., 2011) and sometimes Asian countries, it has concentrated on perception, motivation, disclosure of CSR and impact of the subject on certain privilege stakeholders like the management and shareholders (Rahaman et al., 2000; 2004; Ofori and Hinson, 2007; Hinson, 2010). As many of these studies used some form of content analysis, developed in Western countries, to examine the issue and level of social disclosure in developing countries. There is a real danger in using Western type social reporting methods and techniques in the context of a developing country (Gray et al., 1996).

To add to that, due to different measures that have been applied in assessing the level of disclosures of SR also make generalisations difficult, if not impossible. For example, the use of lines and words as measurements instead of page or paragraph proportion in these previous studies produce different levels of SR. However, these differences are caused by using different tools of measurement rather than actual differences in the level of SR. The main reasons are that the page proportion measurement includes pictorial images, graphs or pie-charts, while counting words and sentences ignores these, therefore perhaps accounting for the lower level of SR in these studies than in those working with page proportions. Other academic papers (Al-Tuwaijri et al., 2004; Cormier et al., 2005; Gray et al., 1995) have researched on whether CSR disclosures are qualitative or quantitative. As far as the researcher can confirm that to the best of his knowledge there is no studies done on the determinants of the level of SR where words, paragraphs and pages have been used at the same time and/or whether entities prepare SR to conform to the informational requirement of their stakeholders have been assessed after proper dialogue especially in mining companies in Ghana. Many studies focused on the disclosure of sustainability information including Frost and Semaer (2002), Marcuccio and Steccolini (2005), Navarro et al. (2010), Farneti and Siboni (2011), Bellringer et al. (2011).

Furthermore, many studies on determinants of environmental performance has been made (see, Christ and Burritt, 2013; Cormier and Magnan, 2003; Cowen et al., 1987; Deegan and Gordon, 1996; Erlandsson and Tillman, 2009; Hackston and Milne, 1996; Liu and Anbumozhi, 2009; Roberts, 1991; Roberts, 1992; Silva Monteiro and Aibar-Guzmán, 2010; Trotman and Bradley, 1981). These studies have examined the effect of corporate characteristic variables such as firm size, profitability, industry, country of reporting, leverage, capital intensity, age of company, the existence of a CSR committee, stakeholder power and governmental influences (Hackston and Milne, 1996; Roberts, 1992). There is no existing empirical knowledge about the effect of these variables on environmental disclosure in Ghana. Therefore, this study will also examine the effects of some of these determinants and environmental disclosure in particular and SR in general.

In the light of the fact that there are no regulatory requirements for the preparation of SR by companies in general and MCGs in Ghana in particular, it is very necessary to assess the level of their sustainability reporting to ascertain the determinant of the level. This study differs from comparable studies on an important aspect, the measurement of sustainability reporting level. Other research has measured the level of disclosure using, the number of words, sentences or pages in the annual report. After this, the relation between specific variables and the amount of disclosures are tested (Deegan and Gordon, 1996; Gray et al., 1995; Guthrie and Parker, 1989; Hackston and Milne, 1996; Milne and Adler, 1999; Neu et al., 1998; Patten, 2002; Burgwal and Vieira, 2014).

Applying this measurement tool, questions can be raised since SR will differ from company to company due to variation in writing style, page and type size (Brammer and Pavelin, 2006; Hackston and Milne, 1996; Burgwal and Vieira, 2014). In addition, there is no straightforward relation between the amount and the level of environmental disclosure. It is more interesting to examine these measures due to the fact that it is highly unlikely for companies to provide adequate information to meet the information requirements of their stakeholders. In view of this the main objective of the study is to find out whether the level of disclosure in SR depend on factors such as size, growth rate, profitability, efficiency, gearing, working capital, age and complexity of the MCG referred to as corporate characteristics. It will be quite interesting, for example, to know whether the content of their various SRs differ in relation to the size of the MCG for example. In effect the study seeks to answer generally;

Whether there is any effect of MCGs' corporate characteristics (size, growth rate, profitability, efficiency, gearing, working capital, age and complexity of the MCG) on the level of sustainability report.

1.3 Evolution of the concept of corporate social responsibility

The phrase corporate social responsibility (CSR) came into being in 1953 after the publication of Bowen's 'Social Responsibility of Businessmen', in which the question such as 'what responsibilities to society can business people reasonably expected to assume' (Drucker, 1984). Businessmen from United States such as Carnegie were among them who brought CSR in the twentieth century. Their views at the time were that companies should not only have profit-making as their main objective but to take the societal well-being into consideration. In view of this the two general principles that came out of these were the charity principle and the steward principle which have been considered as the roots of the modern concept of social responsibility.

The principle of charity is taken to be a situation where less people in the society is taken care by more fortunate people. As time went by companies took over these responsibility when the demand for support grew considerably and it was difficult for individual charities to continue provide such services to the people. This assumption of doing charity work made individual philanthropy to become corporate charity but according to L'Etang, (1995) corporate philanthropy is not synonymous of corporate social responsibility. This is because it is not based on a duty or obligation but on 'the desire to do good' (L'Etang, 1995, p.130). On the other hand with the principle of stewardship, the private corporate managers are known as stewards or trustees to act in the general interest of their shareholders rather than just serving them. Here the managers are considered to be professionals who are expected to act with a certain degree of social responsibility when confronted with business decisions as a result of the position entrusted them by the public.

As noted earlier it is very difficult to have a universally acceptable definition to the evolving concept like CSR. Many terms have been used in connection to the CSR concepts namely corporate citizenship, sustainable business, environmental responsibility, the triple bottom line; social and environmental accountability; business ethics and corporate accountability. In simple terms CSR is the adoption of a set of voluntary policies, codes or guidelines, initiated and driven by the corporation with a certain period of time. Table 1.1 presented some of the definition of CSR. CSR and sustainable development have been considered as having the same aim as both concepts hold the view that business has a moral responsibility to insure that its activities are environmentally sustainable. It is known that companies are established to make profit for the shareholders but effort must be made to ensure that they have the obligation to leave natural ecosystems no worse off in the process of doing businesses. The sustainable development model has the aim of combining the natural constraints established by ecological laws with minimal moral constraints placed upon business activity. In the view of Des Jardins (1998) business activity would be considered as harming the ecosystem when its activities are considered unsustainable or creates wastes that cannot be absorbed by the system. This means that being socially responsible means not only fulfilling legal expectations, but also going beyond compliance and investing 'more' into human capital, the environment and the relations with stakeholders.

Table 1.1 CSR Definitions

Authors	CSR Definitions
Australian Government, Parliamentary Joint Committee on Corporations and Financial Services, (2006).	A company's management of the economic, social and environmental impacts of its activities.
European Union's Green Paper Promoting a European framework for Corporate Social Responsibility, (2001)	A concept whereby companies integrate social and environmental concerns in their business operations and in their interaction with their stakeholders on a voluntary basis.
The Certified General Accountants' Association of Canada, (2005).	A company's commitment to operating in an economically, socially, and environmentally sustainable manner, while recognising the interests of its stakeholders, including investors, customers, employees, business partners, local communities, the environment, and society at large.
The World Bank Group.	The commitment of businesses to contribute to sustainable economic development by working with employees, their families, the local community and society at large to improve their lives in ways that are good for business and for development.
The Business for Social Responsibility Education Fund, (2000).	CSR as operating a business in a manner that meets or exceeds the ethical, legal, commercial, and public expectations that society has of business.

The International standards organisation (ISO).	A balanced approach for organisations to address economic, social and environmental issues in a way that aims to benefit people, communities and society.
The African Institute of Corporate Citizenship.	CSR as the extent to which companies consider and manage their social, environmental and economic impacts and contributions to society as well as the extent to which they do this through stakeholder engagement and reporting on performance.
Richard Holme and Phil Watts, 2000	Continuous commitment by business to behave ethically and contribute to economic development while improving the quality of life of the workforce and their families as well as of the local community and society at large.

Source: SRC Consult, (2010)

Many international organisations, such as the International Organization for Standardisation (ISO), encourage all organisations, not just private ones, to act responsibly. In view of this, the International Council on Mining and Metals commits its members to 'continually seek to improve their performance and contribution to sustainable development so as to enhance shareholder value'. CSR is only one of a number of terms that are used almost inter-changeably to describe this phenomenon. SustainAbility has described CSR as 'helping to prevent the unfolding backlash against globalisation and reverse the recent erosion of trust'. Other expressions that can be used to mean CSR include: 'corporate citizenship', 'corporate accountability' and 'corporate social investment'. Whichever term one chooses to use, the issues that fall under the umbrella of 'CSR' are clear (Salzmann et al., 2005) and include the following:

i. ensuring that the private sector does not contribute to violations of human rights and promotes the respect of these rights;
ii. the respect of core labour standards;

iii. ensuring that local communities benefit from large companies' operations in developing countries;
iv. responsible management of environmental impacts of a company's operations, including emissions, waste and use of sustainable resources;
v. avoidance of corruption and the increase in transparency in business practice;
vi. incorporation of social and environmental criteria in procurement decisions.

Table 1.2 Drivers of Corporate Social Responsibility

1. Globalization with its attendant focus on cross-border trade, multinational enterprises and global supply chains is raising CSR concerns related to human resource management practices, environmental protection, and health and safety.
2. Governments and intergovernmental bodies, such as the United Nations, the Organisation for Economic Co-operation and Development and the International Labour Organization have developed compacts, declarations, guidelines, principles and other instruments that outline social norms for acceptable conduct.
3. Transparency of business activities brought about by the media advances in communications technology, such as the Internet, cellular phones and personal digital assistants are making it easier to track corporate activities and disseminate information about them. Nongovernmental organizations now regularly draw attention through their websites to business practices they view as problematic.
4. Consumers and investors are showing interest in supporting responsible business practices and are demanding more information on how companies are addressing risks and opportunities related to social and environmental issues.
5. Numerous serious and high-profile breaches of corporate ethics have contributed to elevated public mistrust of corporations and highlighted the need for improved corporate governance, transparency, accountability and ethical standards.
6. Citizens in many countries are making it clear that corporations should meet standards of social and environmental care, no matter where they operate.

7. There is increasing awareness of the limits of government legislative and regulatory initiatives to capture all the issues that CSR addresses.
8. Businesses are recognizing that adopting an effective approach to CSR can reduce risk of business disruptions, open up new opportunities, and enhance brand and company reputation.

Source: SRC Consult, (2010)

A number of researches have made on corporate motivations for engaging in sustainability and a case for corporate sustainability (Salzmann et al., 2005). While research on motivations helps provide justification for corporate sustainability initiatives, many studies have shifted from debate as to whether or not corporate sustainability should be implemented to how it can be done in practice (Smith, 2003). Further research have also been made on sustainable supply chain management (Seuring and Muller, 2008), codes of conduct for social responsibility (Bondy et al., 2008), and standardized management systems (Castka and Balzarova, 2008), among other areas. The vast interest on researching in this area is due to the fact that companies expected to behave in environmentally friendly (Bansal and Roth, 2000) and socially friendly (Campbell, 2007) ways. In recent times there is also a growing stream of research on corporate sustainability reporting. Many factors and influences, have led to such increasing attention to CSR in general. Table 1.2 presented some of the drivers of CSR.

1.4 CSR policy and practices in Ghana

In Ghana, as in many countries, companies are not mandated by law to implement CSR activities in the country. The CSR activities are undertaken more in response to moral convictions rather than legal obligations. CSR has evolved slowly from a traditional concept of business philanthropy to the adoption of formal practices, policies and programs in large companies in a number of key sectors. Even though few companies have adopted and internalize practices of CSR in a formal way, many companies in Ghana, particularly large enterprises, are doing everything possible to be socially responsible. The government of Ghana have influence these companies to appreciate CSR by putting in place legislation that defines minimum standards for business performance in terms of policies, laws, practices and initiatives framework. Some of these legislations include constitutional provisions, local government laws and requirements for environmental impact assessments contained in an Act of Parliament. CSR practices have also been encouraged by the government by providing incentives to companies undertaking such activities by granting tax incentives for example to firms that donate for charitable purposes and for sports.

According to Ofori and Hinson (2007) those companies who have some international connection adopt better social responsibilities than the indigenous Ghanaian firms with no international connections. The findings from their studies claimed that the internationally connected companies are more strategic, moral and ethical in their approach to CSR. The indigenous companies and the internationally connected counter parts are rather concentrated on a few select areas such as education, safety, environmental damage, healthcare and consumer protection (Ofori and Hinson, 2007). In the view of Ofori (2006) indigenous companies do not adopt good corporate practices. But Ofori (2007) found that companies that are quoted on the Ghana Stock Exchange are very much aware of their societal obligations and therefore make effort to address most of the concerns raised by their major stakeholders. Most companies in Ghana are aware of the importance as well as the need to adopt CSR practices. On the other hand it seems companies are straddling several divides and sometimes appear that the CSR is not strategically done. According to SRC Consult (2010) 50% of respondents of the studies they conducted in Ghana pay heed to global CSR agreements like the UN Global Compact, whilst others follow local Ghanaian initiatives like the Ghana Business Code. According to the studies the main rationales for CSR practices by such companies are to improve the image of the business and engage in socioeconomic development for the key stakeholders.

In Ghana, companies' CSR concepts revolve around a few major areas: health, cash donations (philanthropy), education, environment, capacity building, company products (philanthropy), and events sponsorship (philanthropy). Some of the factors that motivate CSR selection and design by most companies in Ghana according to SRC (2010) include the needs, interests and expectations of beneficiary communities, companies' resource requirements, and CSR policy and frameworks and guidelines. However, it was realised that although all companies do some form of sustainability reporting but not all companies assess the impact on their CSR practices. One of the main hindrances identified by SRC Consult (2010) is the inadequate allocation of company funds and human resources towards CSR practices by some companies. The study also lamented that many requests from stakeholders, impeded the companies' ability to fully meet the needs of beneficiaries, lack of a sufficiently good insight into the need to be met, and lack of a clear fit between the company's CSR policy and the beneficiary request/need. The companies are then forced to split their resources amongst many competing demands of the stakeholders.

1.5 Sustainability reporting practices

Organisations, in recent times, have been made conscious of impact of their activities on the environmental. In view of this it has become imperative for them to adopt sustainable measures towards the environmental issues for the benefit of their stakeholders. Many researchers have questioned whether sustainable development actually applies to the corporate level (Gray, 2010). This is because the term sustainability development is increasingly being applied under the name of "corporate sustainability" as a corporate concept, even though it is known as a societal concept (Steurer et al., 2005).

According to Gray, (2010) the some of the main arguments against the term "corporate sustainability" are that sustainability is a systems level concept that does not coincide with corporate boundaries and therefore lacks a defined end-state. In spite of this, many organisations are increasingly embarking on corporate sustainability practices (Roca and Searcy, 2012). It is difficult to have one universal definition of corporate sustainability (Roca and Searcy, 2012). IISD, (1992) produced a working definition of corporate sustainability as "adopting business strategies and activities that meet the needs of the enterprise and its stakeholders today while protecting, sustaining, and enhancing the human and natural resources that will be needed in the future" (Roca and Searcy, 2012, p.104). Furthermore, Van Marrewijk (2003) also explains the term to mean the provision of social and environmental concerns in business operations and in interactions with stakeholders (Van Marrewijk, 2003). Another representing definition was given by Dyllick and Hockerts (2002) as: "meeting the needs of the firm's direct and indirect stakeholders (such as shareholders, employees, clients, pressure groups, communities, etc.), without compromising its ability to meet future stakeholder needs as well." This is similar to the definition given by WCED, 1987 (Roca and Searcy, 2012).

According to Roca and Searcy (2012) many researchers have claimed that corporate sustainability is closely associated with CSR. Even though there has been an arguments by many studies that corporate sustainability and CSR are subtly distinct (Van Marrewjick, 2003; Steurer et al., 2005), there are others currently who also consider the two terms as synonyms (Van Marrewijk, 2003). In the view of Steurer et al., (2005) they stated that both corporate sustainability and CSR have converged to similar concepts in recent years" (Steurer et al., 2005). They concluded that both terms have the aim of addressing the economic, environmental, and social dimensions of corporate performance (Steurer et al., 2005) which are referred to by Elkington (1998) commonly as the "triple bottom line" (TBL).

Several names have been used in connection with accounting for sustainability, namely Sustainability Reporting (SR), Social Accounting (SA), Environmental Accounting (EA), Triple-bottom-line (TBL) and Corporate Social Reporting (CSR) (GRI, 2010). Even though there are several definitions of SR there is no universally acceptable one with all the vast literature on the subject. For example, Daub (2007) defines a SR as a report which "must contain qualitative and quantitative information on the extent to which the company has managed to improve its economic, environmental and social effectiveness and efficiency in the reporting period and integrate these aspects in a sustainability management system."

In a similar definition given by the World Business Council for Sustainable Development (WBCSD) SR was defined as "sustainable development reports as public reports by companies to provide internal and external stakeholders with a picture of the corporate position and activities on economic, environmental and social dimensions'" (WBCSD, 2002). According to GRI (2010, p.3), "SR is the practice of measuring, disclosing, and being accountable to internal and external stakeholders for organizational performance towards the goal of sustainable development." This means that SR should be able to provide balanced and reasonable information of the sustainability performance of a reporting organization including both positive and negative contributions. Hubbard (2009) also defined SR as communicating the social, environmental and sustainability performance by the organisation to its stakeholders.

Over the past 30 years SR has been part of the corporate reporting (Owen et al., 2009) and the practice has been on the increase (Smith et al., 2011). There have been an increasing research on sustainability reporting (for example, Kolk, 2003; 2004) but most of these have been dominated by large multinational enterprises (Brown et al., 2009a). Large corporations and multinationals have adopted CSR as a mainstream activity of business (KPMG, 2005). There is also an evidence of an increase in the scope of the reports, a broadening of potential target audiences, an increase in integration with financial reports, and sharpened regional differences in reporting and verification practices (Brown et al., 2009a).

Since 1973 and every three years KPMG produces a survey of environmental reporting patterns of environmental reporting and in 1999 it began to look at sustainability reporting. The early KPMG surveys showed a gradual increase in the proportion of companies surveyed which were producing separate corporate environmental reports, with the percentage arising from 13% in 1993 to 17% (1996), 24% (1999) and 28% (2002). In the 1992 survey indicated that over 30% of the 100 companies sampled in 2002 had incorporated social and economic issues in their environmental reports, thereby moving the environmental reports more towards sustainability.

The main findings of the KPMG (2005) survey were that three years preceding 2005 witnessed a substantial increase worldwide in CSR with a dramatic change from environmental reporting to SR (68% of the top 250 companies in the Fortune 500). The study also revealed that there is an increase in integrated reporting with more information included in annual report (AR) rather than in separate report. The study further revealed that about two-thirds of these reports have corporate governance section and 85% of the reports studied addressed climate change issues. The KPMG (2008) survey confirm an increase in CSR with nearly 80% of the world's largest 250 companies issuing reports, as opposed to 50% in the 2005 survey and now the 'norm' not only for the world's largest companies. The findings also saw climate change reporting increasing but needs to improve substantially. The KPMG (2011) findings showed that CSR had become a 'de facto law' for business and that it 'came of age' in 2011 with 95% of the world largest 250 companies reporting. The research also revealed that two-thirds of companies which were still not reporting on their corporate social responsibility activities were based in the USA.

There has been a considerable increase in reporting by companies in sustainability and corporate responsibility issues rather than only environmental issues through annual reports and stand-alone reports (KPMG, 2002). There are also many survey results that show the growing importance of CSR within the business community. But in spite of all these, there are many questions that needed to be asked. For example, what drives the business community to increasingly report sustainability information? What are the determinants and process of sustainability reporting especially in Ghana? In the views of Adams and McNicholas (2007), there is relatively little information available on the process of developing reports and how they are used (Bartels et al., 2008; Roca and Searcy, 2012). Many studies suggest mixed reasons such as economic and ethical reasons, which echo those suggested in the Western literature (KPMG, 2002, 2005). Interestingly most of the time these surveys are confined to top corporations notably from developed countries (Smith et al., 2011).

There are still no clear explanations of the level of SR in developing countries especially with respect to mining companies. Furthermore, despite the large number of studies of CSR practices in developed countries, there are relatively few studies of CSR practices in developing countries (Lodhia, 2000; 2003; Kuasirikun and Sherer, 2004; Gao et al., 2005). It is also true that reporting practices are no longer restricted to sectors with a high environmental impact in Western countries but also to the non-industrial sector and in other newly industrialised regions (KPMG, 2002; 2005).

During the literature review there were few empirical studies made that tend to explore the possibility of any associations between the preparation of SR and corporate features such as size, growth rate, and corporate performance. The legitimacy and stakeholder theories reviewed showed that few studies have been conducted with respect to whether companies with different characteristics prepare SR to justify their actions towards their stakeholders.

1.6 Conclusion

The chapter presented the concept of corporate social responsibility. It include the grounding assumptions behind the study are reiterated. It also presented the evolution of the Concept of corporate social responsibility and CSR policy and practices in Ghana and Sustainability reporting practices.

CHAPTER 2

Applicable theories of sustainability reporting practices

2.1 Introduction

Chapter provides a chronological review of the existing literature starting with the earliest accounting frameworks providing a critical review of the development of conventional accounting theories namely Stewardship, Managerial Theories, Decision Usefulness Theory, Economic Theories, Accountability Theory, Political Economy Theory (PET), The Stakeholder Theory, and Legitimacy Theory. Furthermore discussions and arguments are presented to provide the theoretical justification relevant to this study.

Researchers have used various theories to explain the reasons behind sustainability reporting practices (Wilmshurst and Frost, 2000; Hooghiemstra, 2000; Buhr, 2001; 2002; Deegan 2002; Deegan et al., 2002; Milne and Patten, 2002; O'Donovan, 2002; O'Dwyer, 2002). There are three groups of theories, each offering different theoretical explanations namely decision usefulness theory, economic theory, and social and political theory that have been suggested by many researchers (Gray et al., 1995a, 1996; Tilt and Symes, 1999). In researching into SR, Gray et al. (1996) further asserted that using system-oriented theories will provide a powerful lens or understanding since it allows the researcher to incorporate a broader societal influences in the analysis of how companies operate and how the information are communicated to the public (Deegan and Unerman, 2006).

The most widely used theories adopted to justify the sustainability reporting practices focus on Legitimacy Theory and Stakeholder Theory (Deegan, 2002; Navarro et al., 2010; Mussari and Monfardini, 2010; Farneti and Siboni, 2011; Garcia-Sanchez et al., 2013). The stakeholder theory (Freeman 1984; Clarkson, 1995; Harrison and Freeman, 1999; Steurer, 2006; Smith et al., 2011) and the legitimate theory (Wood, 1991; Lindblom, 1993; Cormier and Gordon, 2001; Deegan, 2002; Cooper and Owen, 2007) are considered as the most systems-oriented theories used in connection with SR literature. These two theories which look at the effect of corporate operations within a broader social context have been used together with the accountability theory in exploring the research questions of this study. Many studies on SR practices in different countries have used different theoretical perspectives and methods and have engaged in many different research questions (Deegan, 2002).

2.2 Stewardship theory

The term Stewardship is one of the earliest concepts in modern accounting. It is defined as a system where an official is appointed to keep order or supervise the arrangements at a meeting or demonstration or where a person is made responsible for supplies of foods etc. for a college or club for example. From these definitions steward is implicitly expected to use the resources entrusted to him in a responsible manner without providing a detailed account of the way those resources have been used. According to the theory there should be no separation between the functions of the chair and the Chief Executive Officer (CEO).

It has been argued that shareholders interest are maximised when there is a shared incumbency of roles of board chair and CEO (Donaldson and Davis, 1991). Later the separation of ownership and control was given birth to when there was the proliferation of joint stock companies managers were employed to run such companies, on both a short-term and long-term basis. This led to a new class of professionals and a new phenomenon which has been termed by Chandler (1977) as 'managerial capitalism'. Over the years Stewardship has evolved to be the main professional role of managers (Lehman, 1995) and it has compelled companies to report financial information in the form of annual profit, with little attention being paid to non-financial information.

Further work was done by Rechner and Dalton (1991) to examine the relation between CEO duality and organisational performance and it was found that their study supports agency theory expectations about inferior shareholder returns from CEO duality. But when they made a random sample of corporations from the Fortune 500 to identified corporations which had remained as either dual or independent chair-CEO structures for each year of a six-year period (1978–1983) it was found that corporations which had independent chair-CEO structures had higher return on equity (ROE), return on investment (ROI) and profit margins. In their previous work Rechner and Dalton (1989) they found there is no significant difference between structures when they examined the effect of CEO duality on risk adjusted shareholder returns using stock market data for the same sample and period. Thus, there is a need for a further study of shareholder stock market returns further study of the relation of CEO duality and its effects.

2.3 Managerial theories

Managerial theory is one of the theories which emphasized the separation of ownership and control as well as highlighting the concern of owners (Berle and Means, 1932; Gordon, 1945). They were developed as companies grew larger and thereby increasing operational complexity to enhance this separation. The separation of ownership and control meant that managers had more autonomy and incentives to depart from their contracts to pursue their own goals, which were not necessarily the same goals as those of the shareholders (Banard, 1938; Drucker, 1946). Managerial benefits could include salary, security, power, status, prestige, and professional excellence (Williamson, 1963) and managers could achieve their non-profit goals by having a positive preference for expenditures on, for instance, staff and emoluments (Williamson, 1970).

Generally, shareholders do not have either the information on day-to-day operations or the technical and expert knowledge to control managers directly. It is this lack of information which puts managers in a position they could exploit. Formally, this is experienced in the principal agent problems for owners. The principal (owner) has to find ways to make the agent (managers) behave in a way which benefits them (owners). This would be achieved by either policing the agent or designing incentive structures (Coase, 1937). The principal could decide to police the agent if the cost of policing is less than the cost of gathering information to monitor the agent.

The introduction of an incentive mechanism led to managers' interests becoming consistent with those of the shareholders. Managers were given rewards, which were linked to the firm's financial performance. These rewards were in different formats ranging from equity and investment plans (Jensen and Meckling, 1976) to share options (Smith and Watts, 1986). While managerial theories clearly have values in explaining the growth of information disclosure, it is rather limited and fails to recognise information users other than shareholders. Managerial theories are rooted in the existence of an 'economic contract' between principal and agent according to which, companies report financial information to their investors to illustrate that they have acted in their best interests. In the author's view "traditional managerial theories" fail to recognise the possibility of a 'social contract' between companies and other groups and thereby fail to explain why companies might disclose sustainability information. In this way it maintains an isolated view in its analysis and does not consider factors from the external environment.

2.4 Decision usefulness theory

One of the theories used in explaining disclosures is Decision usefulness theory (DUT). The theory argues that organizations disclose information that enables users to make useful decisions. According to this theory, companies disclose social information because certain classes of society such as investors, creditors and shareholders, find it useful in making investment decisions (Dierkes and Antal, 1985; Milne and Chan, 1999). A more general perspective than agency theory uses the concept of decision usefulness of information to a range of information users as well as shareholders. According to this approach, reporting is demand-driven and information should reach each user group to meet their information needs in a satisfactory manner. Most studies on DUT focused on financial information users (Baker and Haslem, 1974; Chenhall and Juchau, 1977; Benjamin and Stanga, 1977). Despite the fact that the main focus of the decision usefulness studies was financial information does not means that sustainability information was not considered a requirements of other stakeholders.

Furthermore, the literature survey implicitly highlights a number of difficulties with respect to DUT. It was realised in the firstly instance that, most studies on this theory failed to provide any explanation of who the information 'user groups' are. Companies are unlikely to simply provide information to any user (or user group) who demands the information. Secondly, there is no clear definition of the term 'usefulness'. What is considered useful to one may not be useful to another. Therefore, the amount of information to be disclosed should not depend on only how a particular stakeholder will find it useful but others needs as well. In addition, SR is not predominated by the needs and wants of, and usefulness to, stakeholders such as shareholders, investors or creditors (Gray et al., 1995a).

2.5 Economic theories

Economic theories are group of two types namely Positive Accounting Theory (PAT) and Economic Agency Theory (EAT) (Ness and Mirza, 1991; Deegan and Hallam, 1991; Milne, 2002). In addition to numerous other rationales (e.g., decision usefulness, legitimacy theory, stakeholder theory, critical or political economy theory (Gray et al., 1995), PAT has been suggested to explain why firms make voluntary social disclosures. The theory tries to make good predictions of real world events and translate them to accounting transactions. Its overall intention is to understand and predict the choice of accounting policies across differing firms As well as recognizing that economic consequences exist. Under PAT, firms want to maximize their prospects for survival, so they organize themselves efficiently. In view of the original work of Watts and Zimmerman (1978, 1986), several empirical studies (e.g., Belkaoui and Karpik 1989; Ness and Mirza, 1991; Panchapakesan and McKinnon, 1992; Lemon and Cahan, 1997) have directly sought to establish evidence for the political cost hypothesis as an explanation for firms' social disclosures. Several related empirical studies have also sought to use the theory to explain other types of voluntary disclosure, including value added statements (Deegan and Hallam, 1991), disclosures by statutory authorities (Lim and McKinnon, 1993), and disclosures in pursuit of reporting excellence awards (Deegan and Carroll, 1993).

According to Watts and Zimmerman (1986, 1990) PAT has three hypotheses around which its predictions are organized namely bonus plan hypothesis, debt/equity covenant hypothesis and political cost or size hypothesis. With bonus plan hypothesis, Ceteris paribus, managers of firms with bonus plans are more likely to choose accounting procedures that shift reported earnings from future periods to the current period. By doing so, they can increase their bonuses for the current year. Debt covenant hypothesis also state that, Ceteris paribus, the closer a firm is to violating accounting-based debt covenants, the more likely the firm manager is to select accounting procedures that shift reported earnings from future periods to the current period. By increasing current earnings, the company is less likely to violate debt covenants, and management has minimized its constraints in running the company. Finally, with the political cost/ size hypothesis, Ceteris paribus, the greater the political costs/ the larger the size of the firm, the more likely the manager are to choose accounting procedures that defer reported earnings from current to future periods.

EAT is directed at the ubiquitous agency relationship, in which one party (the principal) delegates work to another (the agent), who performs that work. Agency theory is concerned with resolving two problems that can occur in agency relationships. The first is the agency problem that arises when (a) the desires or goals of the principal and agent conflict and (b) it is difficult or expensive for the principle to verify what the agent is actually doing. The problem here is that the principal cannot verify that the agent has behaved appropriately. The second is the problem of risk sharing that arises when the principal and agent have different attitudes towards risk. The problem here is that the principal and the agent may prefer different actions because of the different risk preferences. Apart from the debate over the sophistication of EAT and PAT, there is, in fact, much doubt about using these theories to explain SR practices. In particular, these theories do not emphasize 'what should be', they are based on market-based literature and so are entirely contrary to the principle concerns of SR (Gray et al., 1995a).

2.6 Accountability theory

Accountability has been defined by Gray et al. (1991) simply as explaining or justifying what is being done currently and what is planned through the giving of information. Accountability involves, therefore, the giving of information and for that matter providing a report to the stakeholders. According to Gray et al. (1991) organizations are accountable to society at large for their actions and therefore are required to account for the extensiveness to which they complied with the law. They contend that this condition reflects, to a substantial extent, on the distribution of information in general and accounting information in particular among the organization and the individuals, groups and parties in the society.

In their accountability model, Gray et al. (1991; 1996) hypothesise a simple two-way relationship between an accountee and accountor. The Accountee, who they call the 'principal', is the 'shareholder' whereas the Accountor, who they call the 'agent', would be a 'Director' of the organisation in the conventional financial accounting context. In the light of this, it can be deemed that society consists of series of individual social contracts' between members of the society and the society itself that assigns responsibility and right to information. It is also considered that society that determines accountability. The forgoing accountability definitions imply, therefore, that there are three constituents with respect to the idea of accountability namely: (1) the duty to provide an account by those who are accountable (i.e. the provision of information). (2) the responsibility of those who are held accountable for actions and perhaps their consequences: (3) the provision of an account of actions and perhaps their consequences to the accountee (Principal) which might serve as a basis for judgement and assessment by such an accountee, and may affect their decisions.

Many social accounting scholars have proposed that disclosure on social and environmental issues is one of the means through which accountability functions are performed by the organisation because a lot of information is transmitted to a wide variety of stakeholders regarding organisations' social and environmental impacts (Gray, et al., 1996; Unerman, 2000; Adams, 2004; O'Dwyer, et al., 2005; Bouten et al., 2011). Therefore to perform accountability function, however, these disclosures need to demonstrate corporate acceptance of a company's social and environmental responsibility (Adams, 2004). It is true that companies are increasingly disclosing corporate social responsibility information (Archel et al., 2008; Gray et al., 2001; Adams, 2004; Bouten et al., 2011), but the question is whether these information they are disclosing is adequate and the kind of impact they have on the stakeholders (Hopwood, 2009).

There is an increasing awareness over the issue of Corporate Accountability and the need for Sustainability Reporting. In the 1970s, with a clear increase in non-financial information disclosure, the limitation of the 'decision usefulness' approach became clearer. As a result academics sought an alternative to the decision usefulness approach and considered the role of corporate accountability. Conceptually, accountability is a more sophisticated version of stewardship (Gray et al., 1991, p.3), which recognises that companies should have a responsibility to contribute to social welfare as well as a responsibility to serve the owners' interests. In any democratic system, all companies should be accountable not only to their owners but also to society-at-large (Gray et al., 1991) as all individuals have rights to information (Stanton, 1997).

Companies remain unclear about a number of decisions on information disclosure. For instance, the decision on what information categories to disclose is not straightforward nor is the decision on 'who determines the terms of accountability' and 'to whom the accountability is held'. There are differing views on when accountability is due. Tricker (1983) and Stewart (1984) argue that unless the principal can enforce the accountability then there is no accountability, whereas Gray et al. (1996) takes a different view and argue that accountability can exist even if it is not enforceable. This demonstrate why sometimes companies fail to provide information even when they are forced but do provide when they are not forced or obliged to do so. This means that accountability is not necessarily reflected by information disclosure. In this case it could be explained that in a democratic society companies are under moral obligations to fulfil certain tasks that are expected of them. The fact that some certain interested groups do not have the power to demand information shouldn't prevent them from securing information that they need. It should rather be disclosed on grounds of rights to information by referring to the natural and moral rights but not only to the legal requirements.

Organisations have used accounts to disclose information to their stakeholders. Currently, such 'accounts' are predominantly financial and are geared towards the most powerful stakeholders (Gray et al., 1996). Information reported by companies should not be made for the benefit of only the most powerful stakeholders but must address issues of interest to a wide range of stakeholders. In the absence of legal and regulatory requirements for sustainability information disclosure, the way companies predominately concentrate on financial information and disclose sustainability information on voluntary basis, suggest that companies do not discharge their accountability to their society. They disclose information for reasons other than discharging their accountability to their society.

2.7 Political economy theory (PET)

Political economy theory is one of the Social and political theories that form the basis of this study mainly due to the demerits associated with the other groups of theories described above. The social and political theories dual on the relationship between businesses, individual groups and the state on which, accountability of corporations can be addressed (Gray et al., 1995a; 1996). They are the group of theories in which the social power of organizations is emphasized, specifically in its relationship and responsibility with society and political arena associated with this power. This leads the corporation to accept social duties and rights and to participate in certain social cooperation (Gray et al., 1996).

The PET therefore suggest a interrelationship between political and economic forces in accounting practice and how they act to provide the necessary information for decision making that allows for the exercise of power (Miller, 1991). The PET is one theoretical framework that was developed with the aim to articulate the changes, pressures and factors emanating from the external environment (Gray et al., 1996). Rather than focusing upon the concerns of shareholders and managers, the PET emphasizes the importance of accounting information to secure power relationship in society. It argues that accounting information can influence the distribution of income, wealth and power in any society (Lukes, 1974). The political economy theory has two branches namely Classical Political Economy Theory (CPET) and Bourgeois Political Economy (BPET) (Gray et al., 1996).

The CPET is concerned with structural conflict, inequality and the role of state (Gray, et al., 1995a; Gray et al., 1996). According to this theory, the social system encourages companies to disclose non-financial information (Puxty, 1991) with the state playing a central role. The theory focuses on well-defined groups within society and their interaction within the social system and its power relations that leads to information disclosure. Individual companies and agents are only important as members of particular social groups. CPET is sometimes called conflict-based framework. The BPET the other hand, views the world as a pluralist, in the sense that power is believed to be diffused with individual preferences determining social choices with no one individual having the power to influence society. It therefore emphasizes the relationships between companies and individuals or groups of individuals', whereby the power associated with individuals or groups of individuals compels companies to provide sustainability information.

The proponents of both CPET and BPET present views at the two opposing extreme ends of political economy spectrum. According to Gray et al., (1988), a large proportion of the literature on the issue of corporate social responsibility, which was an important area for the development of theories in the 1980s, adopts what they call a "middle-ground thinking" and falls within the framework of the bourgeois political economy. In spite of the criticisms of the BPET, the theory provides a more suitable theoretical framework for the analysis of sustainability information disclosures by companies. The two branches of BPET are stakeholder and legitimacy theories and these have been explained in the subsequent Sections below.

2.8 Stakeholder theory

According to Freeman's (1984) stakeholder was defined as "any group or individual who can affect or is affected by the achievement of the organization's objectives" (p.157). Stakeholder theory states that organisations have many stakeholders who include not only shareholders but also employees, communities, creditors, customers, government and investors (Freeman, 1984). There is the need therefore for organisations to manage its relationship with its many stakeholders (Freeman, 1984) and to manage such relationships involve different arguments. These arguments lead to a number of variations of this theory. Proponents of theory believe that although the organisation has the responsibility of increasing the share value of its investors, it should also take into consideration the numerous others who have a stake in its existence (Freeman, 1984; Deegan, 2002; Smith et al., 2011).

The stakeholder theory is one of the theories often used by researchers in the system-oriented framework in SR literature (Freeman, 1984; Evans and Freeman, 1993; Clarkson, 1995; Harrison and freeman, 1999; Steurer, 2006; Smith et al., 2011). One reason for this frequent use is that the theory focuses on the effect of the activities of organisations on all the stakeholders (Smith et al., 2011). Stakeholder theory provides an explanation of how organisations can manage their stakeholder groups (Deegan and Unerman, 2006; 2008). Theorists in accounting discipline, specifically social accounting, have classified stakeholder theory into two main subdivisions namely the managerial (instrumental) and the ethical (normative) stakeholder theory (Deegan and Unerman, 2006; 2008; Donaldson and Preston, 1995; Jamali et al., 2008; Freeman et al., 2010; Mahadeo et al., 2011).

The managerial stakeholder theory looks at the organisations' relationships with different stakeholders, the nature of those relationships, the outcomes for both, and the process of strategic stakeholder management (Caroll and Buchholtz, 2006). The managerial stakeholder theory there is the need to control stakeholders who are deemed to have a more direct and critical impact on the company (Mitchell et al., 1997; Roberts, 1992; Ullman, 1985; Mahadeo et al., 2011) and have the ability to withdraw resources destined for the company and thereby endanger its existence. Therefore to ensure stakeholders continued support to meet corporate objectives there is the need to manage them (Mahadeo et al., 2011). Freeman et al. (2010, p.8) claimed that the managerial stakeholder theory offers a managerial perspective on how business works at its best. One main demerit of the theory is that it focuses mainly on the expectations of primary rather than secondary stakeholders, in other words, stakeholders who are fundamental for the existence and survival of the organisation (Clarkson, 1995). Proponents of this theory identify relevant stakeholders based on the attributes of legitimacy, power and urgency (Mitchell et al., 1997).

With the case of ethical stakeholder theory the organisations have the duty to give accounts of their operations, for example, preparation of SR can be seen as an accountability mechanism in that it reflects an organization's duty to account for its actions (Mahadeo et al., 2011). According to Mahadeo et al. (2011) managerial stakeholder theory has attracted the most attention in the SR literature. This implies that companies have identified their target audience and are providing information that will influence (or distract) this group (Gray et al., 1996; Mahadeo et al., 2011).

The view portrayed by the managerial stakeholder theory is challenged by researchers working within the normative branch. These researchers argue that the managerial perspective of stakeholder theory is only concerned with how the organisation manages its powerful stakeholders (Gray et al., 1996), with the aim of building or maintaining its legitimacy (Gray et al., 1997; Mitchell et al., 1997). The theory considers "specifically different stakeholder groups within society and how they should best be managed if the organisation is to survive" (Deegan and Unerman, 2006; 2008, p.289). The main argument of these researchers is that all the types of stakeholders namely primary and secondary, should be considered by management since they have certain minimum rights that must not be taken for granted, and issues of stakeholder power (legitimacy and agency) are not important (Deegan and Unerman, 2006; 2008, p.287).

In the view of Donaldson and Preston (1995) there are three variants of the stakeholder theory: the normative, the instrumental, and the descriptive variants. The normative variant of stakeholder theory states that management should solve stakeholder problems from an accountability perspective. The normative stakeholder perspective further explains that companies do have a duty and obligation to wider society and corporations, and are perhaps, obliged to make social disclosure in order to discharge wider accountability by providing accounts to relevant stakeholders (Gray et al., 1996; Buhr, 2001). It provides guidance as to how an organisation should treat its stakeholders (Deegan, 2002). From the normative perspective of stakeholder theory, an important consideration is that the impact of organisations' objectives and activities on the lives of stakeholders (and here the environment, non-human species, and future generations should be included) "should be what determines the organisation's responsibilities to that stakeholder rather than the existence of that stakeholder's economic power over the organisation" (Deegan and Unerman, 2006; 2008, p.286). This normative view claims that all stakeholders have intrinsic rights.

The claim by Deegan and Unerman (2006; 2008) that should be right to live in a clean environment, with safe working conditions and fair salaries, have informed how an organisation impacts the stakeholders, even if they choose not to use the information (O'Dwyer, 2005). In view of this claim, it can be inferred that the normative branch of stakeholder theory is based on accountability. Therefore the duty to take responsibility to embark upon certain actions needs to be accounted for in line with those actions (Gray et al., 1996). Deegan and Unerman (2006; 2008) concluded that it is the need to be accountable that should drive the actions of companies, rather than the need to respond to primary stakeholders to ensure the survival of the organisation. Therefore this means that the normative branch of stakeholder theory is concern how companies should act, which is not the same as how organisations actually act.

The instrumental and descriptive stakeholder theory variants also look at how the organisations should manage those stakeholders considered powerful by identifying them with the self-interest of the business (Donaldson and Preston, 1995; Woodward et al., 1996; Gray et al., 1996; 1997). These variants help to explain the reason why organisations produce SR to fulfil the corporate accountability from the positive to the normative. In view of this, sustainability reports are prepared for those stakeholders that appeared to be important to the company. According to Gray et al. (1996) information can be employed by the organisation to manipulate the stakeholder in order to gain their support and approval, or to distract their opposition and disapproval. This means that the two variants are of the view that companies will prepare SR to manage the perception of stakeholders who are considered to be powerful not actually to demonstrate accountability but to gain approval and support for the business to exist (Adler and Milne, 1997; Deegan, 2002). It can therefore be concluded that companies who want to maintain a good relationship with its different stakeholders should prepare SR.

The stakeholder theory has suffered a lot of critiques by many writers. Philips (1997) criticized it by arguing that it is too broad and all-inclusive to the extent that even terrorists can be considered as stakeholders since their action also can affect the company. He used the idea of the principle of fairness to keep some groups, such as terrorists, out of the stakeholder group. Donaldson (1989) also criticized the theory, despite its insights, that it has serious problems. The two most obvious are its inability to provide standards for assigning relative weight to the interest of various constituencies, and its failure to contain within itself, or make reference to, a normative, justificatory foundation. Another significant critique of the theory is that it implies neutral relationships between the stakeholders, because it focuses almost exclusively on the relationship between the company, and stakeholders or stakeholder groups, rather than the extent and manner in which stakeholders can be involved in decision-making. In a study by Mahadeo et al. (2011), outlined a calculated and focused responsiveness of companies to a defined audience of stakeholders to majority of the stakeholder groups tend to be the commercially (or financially) motivated ones. In the view of Cormier et al. (2004), Islam and Deegan (2008), Elijido-Ten et al. (2010), and Huang and Kung (2010) suppliers, customers, lenders, competitors and investors but relatively less on the public, governments, employees and communities (Tilt, 1994).

2.9 Legitimacy theory

The difference between stakeholder theory and legitimacy theory appears to be less tied to the assumption of discrete and identifiable factions of stakeholders (Mahadeo et al., 2011). Suchman (1995), defined legitimacy as a state where an organization's actions are seen to be "... desirable, proper or appropriate within some socially constructed system of norms, values, beliefs and definitions" (1995, p. 574). The Legitimacy theory states that organisation as social construct have a social contract with society and what mandate them to continue in operation will only be the situation where their actions are seen as legitimate (Deegan, 2003, 2007; Deegan and Unerman, 2007; 2008; Smith et al., 2011; Mahadeo et al., 2011). According to Mahadeo et al. (2011) legitimacy entrust the organization the power to engage in and control the processes of legitimation to demonstrate its congruence with societal values. Legitimacy, like an intangible asset, is seen as an operational resource (Suchman, 1995; Tilling and Tilt, 2010; Mahadeo et al., 2011) whose value must be maintained to ensure continued support from society. This means that companies need to secure legitimacy in order to be accepted by society. In view of this organisations need to create strategies to "ensure that their activities are perceived by society as being legitimate" (Deegan and Unerman, 2006; 2008, p.271). Where such legitimacy is not seen or when the organisation's value systems are not congruent with the social systems then the legitimacy will be negatively affected (Haniffa and Cooke, 2005; Lindblom, 1993, 2010; Suchman, 1995 as quoted in Smith et al., 2011). In other words, organisations that exhibit a poor economic, social and environmental performance will find it difficult to obtain the "license to operate" in society (Lindblom, 2010). Failure by the organisation to meet the social contract may lead to penalties such as legal sanctions, limited resources, and reduced demand for their products (Lindblom, 2010, p.52).

The society is of the view that organisations should not only focus on the provision of benefits to their investors but to consider providing benefits for society as a whole (Deegan and Unerman, 2006; 2008, p.272). According to Mathews (1993) organisations operate with the help of the social contract. This principle of social contract means that Society, as a collection of individuals, provides organisations with their legal standing, the authority to own and the use natural resources as well as to hiring of its labour force. Organisations draw on community resources and output both goods and services and waste products to the general environment. The organisation has no inherent rights to these benefits, and in order to allow their existence, society would expect the benefits to exceed the costs to society (Deegan and Unerman, 2006; 2008, p.272).

Legitimacy theory is also said to provide an explanation of the means whereby organisations seek to gain legitimacy in society (Deegan and Unerman, 2006; 2008). Therefore, legitimation is the process whereby an organization justifies to a superordinate system its right to exist, that is, to continue to import, transform, and export energy, material or information

(Maurer, 1971). The theory is adopted to explain why the preparation of voluntary social and environmental reporting (Wilmshurst and Frost, 2000; Deegan et al., 2000, 2002; Deegan, 2002; 2002a; O'Donovan, 2002; Milne and Patten, 2002; Mobus, 2005; Rayman-Bacchus, 2006). For companies to continue to survive and grow, they have to perform well and undertake various socially desirable actions, including distribution of economic, social, or political benefits to the groups from whom they derive their power (Shocker and Sethi, 1973). As far as companies are concerned, it is important that society recognises the compatibility of their behaviour with its ethical values (Dowling and Pfeffer, 1975). If a company fails to operate within the boundaries set by the social norms, the society may revoke its contract and prevent it continuing its operations (Deegan and Rankin, 1996).

Using the legitimacy perspective, firms voluntarily disclose social and environmental information to show that they are conforming to the expectations and values of the society within which they operate. The theory assumes that the business enterprise must appear to consider the rights of the public at large and not only the rights of its investors. The theory further explains why the agent (organisation) should disseminate some information to the principal (society) (Kokubu et al., 1994). Therefore, legitimacy theory emphasizes the management purpose and its power over information and how such information can be disseminated in the form of a report to its stakeholders.

Legitimacy theory has been subjected to empirical testing by several research studies conducted in the area of CSR (Deegan et al., 2000; O'Dwyer, 2002; Campbell et al., 2003; Ahmad and Sulaiman, 2004; Rahaman, et al., 2004; Smith et al., 2011). It is also worth noting that legitimacy theory is the dominant research theory on why business organisations disclose CSR information (Jenkins, 2004). Deegan et al. (2002) also attest to this fact by alluding that the theory appears to be the most frequently used theory in social and environmental disclosure research. As compared to stakeholder theory, the dissemination of CSR information is at the discretion of management and, therefore, ignore the right of many other stakeholders to receive, and the obligation of an organization to provide (i.e. disclose) this type of information. Deegan and Rankin (1996) suggest that social expectation no longer rests upon mere generation of profit but has broadened to include health and safety of employees and local communities as well as concern for the natural environment. Brown and Deegan (2002) noted that social expectation may change over time so organisations need to continually maintain their legitimacy (O'Donovan, 2002).

There are various strategies that companies can use to disclose social information to proof their own existence (Brown and Deegan, 1998). The following four possible strategies, as identified by Lindblom (1994; 2010, pp.57-60) can be explored in the legitimation process;

1. to seek to educate and inform its 'relevant publics' about actual changes in its performance and activities, hence closing the gap;
2. to seek to change the perceptions of the relevant public without changing the organisations' way of doing things;
3. to seek to manipulate perception by diverting attention from what seems to be the issue of concern to other related issues through an appeal to, for example, emotive symbols;
4. to seek to change external expectations of performance.

Each of these strategies can be used to change the perception or expectation of society with or without changing the real activities of the firm (Milne and Patten, 2002). Milne and Patten (2002) state that legitimation may actually mean very little in terms of significant change in activities of the organisation. Lindblom (2010, p.52) is of the view that organisations may seek to achieve a status of legitimacy, that is, "a condition or status which exists when an entity's value system is congruent with the value system of the larger social system of which the entity is a part". The legitimacy process is said to be controlled by institutional pressure rather than by the manager. In view of this companies, according to Milne and Patten (2002) report social information in order to conform to social, environmental and political institutional pressure. Milne and Patten (2002) describe such reporting as a strategy 'to inform' rather than 'to involve or act'. The institutional approach assumes that managers' encounter pressure from different institutions in society (Deegan, 2002) and this compel them to conform to norms that are largely imposed upon them.

The legitimacy and stakeholder theories are the most relevant and appropriate theories that explain the SR practices by companies according to the literature review. One of the shortcomings of the literature review on the empirical studies on the preparation of SR in the context of legitimacy theory is that it focuses on the way companies divulge information in response to major social and environmental incidents. The literature tends to ignore other potential factors that can put companies under pressure to prepare SR. According to Lindblom, (2010), companies whose practices or actions do not conform to those of society are likely to prepare SR in an attempt either to justify or to divert public attention, or to change and/or manipulate external expectations. In the view of the researcher, the deviation from social norms and values could be due to reasons, which stem from corporate characteristics (e.g. Size, growth rate and performance).

Regardless of the common perception that preparation of SR is made to legitimize their practices there is also the move towards transparency to conform to their stakeholders' information requirement Elkington (1999). However, the researcher is of the view that, these companies operate in a constantly changing external environment and therefore need to exhibit certain degree of flexibility to maintain responsiveness to the changing stakeholders' values and expectations. Contrary to the views of Ball et al. (2000) there has been a failure of external verifiers to ensure the quality of environmental reports in a manner that it is expected to protect the interests of stakeholders.

The legitimacy theory is probably the most widely used to explain environmental disclosure (Burgwal and Vieira, 2014). According to Cho and Patten (2007), the legitimacy theory implies that social and environmental disclosure is a function of the extent of pressure receives from societal and political regarding the environmental performance. This encourages companies to prepare SR to provide more environmental information as a result of these pressures. There is a, so-called, social contract between the organization and the society and if the society observes that the organization fails to operate within the conditions of the contract in accordance with the societal values, there will be a negative societal opinion about this organization (Milne and Patten, 2002; and Burgwal and Vieira, 2014). In such a manner that does not satisfy the society, it will break the organization's social contract. The societal reaction will be, for example, reduced demand by consumers for the products or services from the organization, and suppliers will limit the supply of resources to the firm (Deegan, 2002). There is a legitimacy gap when the social contract is broken. In the light of this, organizations will do the best to repair or compensate the broken contract (Deegan, 2002) by providing, for example, positive sustainability report (Milne and Patten, 2002; Patten, 1992).

There are three main implications of legitimate theory from the above explanation. In the first place, the norms, values and beliefs of society are not fixed over time; legitimacy is a dynamic construct with the organization responding to new imperatives and discarding previously held perceptions (see, Tilling and Tilt, 2010; De Villiers and Van Staden, 2006).

Secondly, theory represents an overall evaluation of social norms, beliefs and expectations and may not be influenced by particular events, but rather by a history of events (Suchman, 1995). Thirdly, society needs to be informed about the actions or activities adopted by the organization since this is a crucial element of the legitimation process (Deegan, Rankin, and Voght, 2000; Dowling and Pfeffer, 1975; Lindblom, 1994; Newson and Deegan, 2002). According to Mahadeo et al. (2011) these implications reinforce the view that legitimacy-based studies need to focus on the broader social, economic and political factors and how these might affect SR practices over a period of time rather than focusing on only one point in time. Previous studies of social and environmental reporting practices (see, Deegan, Rankin, and Tobin, 2002; Parker, 2005; Stanton and Stanton, 2002; Mahadeo et al., 2011) conclude that patterns of disclosure over time or the variability in disclosures between companies can be explained by legitimacy theory (e.g., size and industry effect). On the other hand there have been inconsistent findings (see, for example, Campbell et al., 2003; O'Dwyer, 2002; Owen, 2008; as quoted by Mahadeo et al., 2011).

2.10 Voluntary disclosure theory (VDT)

Explanation from legitimacy theory and stakeholder theory suggest that the two theories are useful in explaining 'what' being disclosed, but not useful in explaining 'how much' disclosure an organisation can make (Clarkson et al., 2008; and Burgwal and Vieira, 2014). Therefore, VDT, based on the agency theory perspective a supplementary theory, is used in the literature to explain the level of disclosure practices. According to Brammer and Pavelin (2006, p.1171; quoted in Burgwal and Vieira, 2014): "Voluntary disclosures are attempts to remove informational asymmetries between the firm and external agents, primarily agents in the investment community." The VDT states that organizations will not hide social and environmental impact of their operations and are will be willing to inform stakeholders about their environmental activities which have a good environmental performance (Burgwal and Vieira, 2014).

Study made by Brammer and Pavelin (2006) concluded that voluntary disclosure suggests that the information risk for current and potential investors will be lowered (Brammer and Pavelin, 2006; Burgwal and

Vieira, 2014). According to the study there are two main reasons for these assertions. In the first place, voluntary disclosure can lead to a competitive advantage because it highlights the environmental programs and the impact of activities on the natural environment by the company. Secondly, both bad and good news are received by stakeholders at almost the same time. On the other hand, if there is low or no disclosure, stakeholders will assume that the current environmental strategy adopted by the firm is inferior to companies that disclose such information (Clarkson et al., 2008; Verrecchia, 1983; Burgwal and Vieira, 2014).

2.11 The theoretical application and justification

There have been many theoretical frameworks used in explaining the concept of sustainability practices. Both the legitimacy and stakeholder theories analyse CSR from different perspectives and as is discussed above, a number of empirical studies have been carried out to find evidence in support of the two theories. Stakeholder theory (Freeman, 1984) is the most prominent of these theoretical frameworks. The theory asserts that organizations have obligations to many individuals and groups (shareholders, customers, and employees, among others) that affect and are affected by the organization (Freeman, 1984). According to Donaldson and Preston (1995) the stakeholder theory is fundamentally normative, though it does also include descriptive and instrumental aspects. The influence of stakeholder theory on corporate sustainability practices is evident from the definitions of corporate sustainability practices. Legitimacy theory (Suchman, 1995) has also been cited in several papers on corporate sustainability reporting. Legitimacy may be defined as "a generalized perception or assumption that the actions of an entity are desirable, proper, or appropriate within some socially constructed system of norms, values, beliefs, and definitions" (Suchman, 1995). Whilst the legitimacy theory seeks to explain the reasons why companies disclose sustainability information to their stakeholders, stakeholder theory identifies various stakeholder groups. It can, in view of this explanation be admitted that these theories are in many ways complementary rather than opposed (Adams and Whelan, 2009).

Some researchers argued that although legitimacy theory provides a base to explain the reasons behind the adoption of sustainability practices &stakeholder theory focusing mainly on organisations having different stakeholder groups, there are some questions to be answered (Deegan,

2000; Deegan and Unerman, 2006; 2008). According to Deegan (2002, p.295), for example, legitimacy theory provides "poor resolution" in that it talks about society as a whole; therefore, it fails to examine specific civil society groups, their power and their influence on other groups and as well as their influence on the organisations. With respect to stakeholder theory the study further explains that the theory addresses this issue by accepting that "different groups have different views about how organisations should conduct their operations, and have different abilities to affect an organisation (Deegan, 2002).

It can be stated following the above argument that there are strong links between Legitimacy Theory and Stakeholder Theory. Legitimacy Theory is about compliance with the expectations of society as implied within the social contract (Richardson, 1997). Society is made up of various groups with different degrees of power or ability to influence the activities of an organization. Stakeholder Theory acknowledges that different groups have different abilities to affect an organization and be affected (Guthrie and Parker, 1989; Davidson, 1991). As Freeman (1984) alluded, Stakeholder Theory is based on the idea that every organization has many counterparts, apart from their owners who depend and are depended by the organisation. In this view, the theory may help managers to identify which stakeholder groups might be relevant and what expectations should be taken into account by the organization to stay within its social contract. Therefore, it behoves on organisations to report to all these stakeholders, and to expand organizations' functions and responsibility apart from their focus on shareholders' needs (Roberts, 1992).

In the view of Garcia-Sanchez et al. (2013), there is a connection between Legitimacy Theory and Stakeholder Theory to confirm the above assertion. According to Stakeholder Theory, as organizations are depending on the environment for resources, they are expected to employ strategies to manage their stakeholders in order to have continued access to the resources which are important to their survival (Garcia-Sanchez et al., 2013). In the same vain, Legitimacy Theory suggests that when managers consider a resource to be critical to firm survival, they will need to adopt measures and strategies to ensure the continued availability of that resource. Therefore, both Stakeholder Theory and Legitimacy Theory portray an organization as dependent on society for resources critical to entities' survival (Garcia-Sanchez et al., 2013).

A number of theoretical frameworks have been used to explore corporate sustainability reporting practices. Deegan (2002) points out that since social and environmental accounting still does not have an accepted theory, there is thus much variation in the theoretical perspectives of researchers to undertake in explaining the motivations behind CSR. This makes researchers to use more than one theory. Deegan (2002) also stated that there could be several reasons behind the use of more than one theory on CSR and each theory provides a slightly different and useful insight into CSR practices. However, some academics do not support this kind of strategy but are of the view that a researcher should adopt and use just one view of the world (Deegan, 2002). They demonstrate that stakeholder and legitimacy theory are based on a bourgeois political economy explanation and both come from a partially common place such as neo-pluralist explanation of society. Therefore both theories are adopted in this study to enhance the understanding of sustainability reporting practices, rather than using a single theory since they seem to accept the explanation of classical political economy theory.

One of the main advantage of using both theories (legitimacy and stakeholder theory) in social accounting other than one theory is that as they are useful to interpret sustainability practices in a developed country, it seems of even more useful in explaining sustainability practices in developing countries for example in Ghana in general and mining companies in particular. Therefore with reference from Woodward et al. (2001) study uses theoretical lenses from stakeholder theory and legitimacy theory within the wider framework of global political economy. Woodward et al. (2001) suggest that the attitude of executives regarding social responsibility suggests both legitimacy and a political economy explanation can be utilized to analyse those responses.

Furthermore, it has been suggested the concept of corporate legitimacy and the move towards corporate transparency are potentially contradictory. This is seen in the previous studies (see Gray, 1997; Adams, et al., 1995) which suggest a rise in the quantity rather than the quality of SR do indicates the increasing use of CSR information by companies for legitimacy purposes. This is said to undermine the underlying issues of stakeholder dialogue and informational needs in relation to the quality of sustainability information. Again, the concentration of existing literature on social, economic and environmental incidents to argue that companies disclose the relevant information to justify their behaviours offers little evidence to suggest that the disclosure of such information even when no social or environmental incident has occurred in the absence of statutory or legal requirements for companies to report freely.

Even though this study uses legitimacy theory as its main theoretical theme, stakeholder theory was also used jointly and interchangeably along with legitimacy theory in order to explain the evidence that will be observed on the research questions. This is in agreement by the claim by researchers (Gray, et al., 1997) that the two theories supplement each other's shortcomings when they are used. For example it can be deduced from the previous Sections that legitimacy theory recognises neither the existence of different stakeholder nor the importance companies attach to them but conform their actions to legitimise their existence. On the contrary, stakeholder theory fails to argue that companies may prepare SR to legitimise their actions but do recognise the different and importance of stakeholders. In this vain, the two theories provide a stronger theoretical framework for the study by supplementing each other. The legitimacy theory will be used to discuss the first three research questions which look at the relationship of the SR and the MCGs characteristics; stakeholder theory will be used to discuss whether there is consultation and dialogue between the organisation and the stakeholders when preparing the SR in terms of adequacy and quality. Therefore the two theories will be used jointly and inter-changeably, although with more weight being attached to legitimacy theory.

Another justification for the application of these theories is that there is one practical problems with legitimacy theory in the sense that its place emphases on the society at large which is considered to be too broad. In this vain the theory fails to identify different groups that form society-at-large and, therefore, does not provide a detailed analysis of the relationship between companies and each group to show how powerful some of these groups might be in provoking companies to disclose such information. These pave the way for a theory that identifies different groups in society and recognises the existence of different stakeholders. Companies could prepare SR in order to justify their actions to their different interest groups, who are commonly known as stakeholders. Stakeholder theory identifies stakeholders as individuals, or groups of individuals, who have legitimate interest in a company. Some stakeholder groups are of more importance to their companies than others are, depending on the importance attached to the resources they control.

The MCGs may use SR to satisfy the information requirements of their stakeholders by adopting the second, the third or the fourth strategies, introduced by Lindblom (2010) without paying much attention to its quality. Lindblom (1993; 2010) in his strategies stated that companies can be made to prepare SR to justify their actions towards satisfying their stakeholders. The MCGs need to identify their stakeholders as well as holding a dialogue with them to seek their information requirements in the absence of any regulatory requirements. Stakeholder theory identifies stakeholders as individuals, or groups of individuals, who have legitimate interest in a company. It has been realised for the forgoing Sections that proponents of legitimacy theory, considered companies as operating in an external environment which are constantly changing and they must endeavour to ensure that their operations are within the bounds and norms of their respective societies. This means that the preparation of SR is a direct response to environmental factors (Preston and Post, 1975) and therefore employed as a means of justifying corporate actions as well as projecting their core values and ideas (Dierkes and Antal, 1985; Deegan, et al., 2000).

The level of sustainability information to be produced tend to vary depending on the results of certain corporate factors of MCGs. The stakeholders and for that matter society is increasingly expecting and demanding from MCGs to respond to constantly changing social, economic and environmental standard. MCGs can also report information in response to the occurrence of particular incident(s) such as an environmental disaster that puts them in the spotlight. In order to achieve the approval of society and to have their survival guaranteed MCGs are required to release sustainability information that is sufficient in terms of both quality and quantity (Woodward, et al., 1996) to satisfy the information requirement of their stakeholders. Most theoretical literature depict that many companies prepare sustainability report to justify their actions to their stakeholders and to ensure conformity with what is known to be socially acceptable. There is also empirical literature that suggests that the occurrence of certain events affect the level of sustainability reporting. Some of the findings of the main empirical studies of legitimate theory have been reviewed in this study as follows:

One of the studies by Honger (1982) confirms that there is evidence suggesting that social reporting was, indeed, in response to society's expectations of corporate behaviour. Within the same decade Guthrie and Parker (1989) had longitudinal studies to review of the disclosed social information over a period of one hundred years commencing 1885 and were also found there was no evidence of disclosure in response to economic, social or political conditions or events.

Deegan and Gordon (1996) on their research on environmental reporting in annual reports of the Australian companies between 1980 and 1991 to assessed the association between environmental disclosures and concern held by environmental groups in particular industry. They found that there is positive association between the level of membership of environmental groups and the disclosure of environmental information. They concluded that companies in certain industries for example mining disclosed more environmental information. A study conducted by Deegan and Rankin (1996) on the same environmental reporting in the corporate annual reports of a sample of Australian firms that were successfully prosecuted for breached of various environmental protection laws during the period 1990 and 1993 were also found that there was significant increase in the disclosure of environmental information when firms are facing environmental prosecution.

According to Wilmshurst and Frost (2000) there was supporting evidence that management responds to the perceived importance of stakeholders hence meeting the information needs of the general community and stakeholders. This was as a result of studies done to find out the possibility of association between factors perceived as important by Chief Finance Officers in the decision to disclose environmental information within the annual report of selected Australian companies was examined. A research by Deegan, et al. (2000) also looked at the reactions of Australian firms in terms of annual reports disclosure to five major incidents were examined. It was also found that companies change their disclosure policies around the time of major company and industry events. In other words disclosures appear to be related to an event rather than related to the social issues.

The phenomenon of sustainability reporting otherwise known as corporate social and environmental disclosure has attracted research attention from many different points of view (Gray et al., 2001). This increasing phenomenon might be expected to attract research attention for its own sake especially given the very significant attention paid to the production of environmental. According to Gray et al. (2001) studies concerned with the decision-usefulness of corporate reporting have regularly reported social and environmental disclosures emanating from decision significance (see, for example, Benjamin and Stanga, 1977; Belkaoui, 1984;

Firth, 1978, 1979 and 1984; Dierkes and Antal, 1985; and Epstein and Freedman, 1994) except see McNally et al., (1982) who presented a contrary view to that assertion. Researchers employing legitimacy theory have seen such disclosures as an important element in the corporation's maintenance of its freedom, status and reputation with influential publics or stakeholders (see, for example, Abbott and Monsen, 1979; Hogner, 1982; Gray et al., 2001; and Roberts, 1992). Thus a substantial body of literature from a wide spectrum of theoretical positions concludes that SRs are an important phenomenon employed by corporations for a variety purposes. Although there are significant differences within that literature, it can be concluded that we should expect to find that larger and higher-profile companies exhibit a greater predisposition towards the use of social and environmental disclosures (Gray et al., 2001).

In conclusion the stakeholder and legitimacy theory are highly interrelated with one another in the sense that whereas the legitimacy theory focuses on communication with society, the stakeholder theory focuses on the communication with different stakeholder groups (Burgwal and Vieira, 2014). Stakeholder theory, as known above, states that society consists of various stakeholder groups who have unequal power to influence the activities of an organization in relation to their social and environmental performance (Roberts, 1992; and Burgwal and Vieira, 2014). In view of this it is expected that the corporate activities are adjusted to conform to the demands of stakeholders (Gray et al., 1995), because stakeholders have the ability to control resources that are critical for the activities of an organization (Ullmann, 1985; and Burgwal and Vieira, 2014). According to Roberts (1992) observes that disclosure is part of the dialogue between the company and its stakeholders for negotiating the social contracts. Therefore, legitimacy and stakeholder theory are closely related and should not be considered competing but in a broader sense as complementing each other (Deegan, 2002; O'Donovan, 2002; Burgwal and Vieira, 2014).

2.12 Conclusion

This Chapter was used to review the most of the accounting literature relating to different theories to explain the disclosure of sustainability information over the years. After a critical review of these literatures it was found that despite its valuable contribution in broadening our understanding of information disclosure, there is the need for a wider perspective for the purpose of giving consideration to the various elements from the external environment in which companies operate. The theory that was considered in this direction was the bourgeois political economy theory which adopts a pluralist view of the world and emphasises the relationships between companies and individuals/groups. The literature review conducted revealed that the theory considers power to be diffused and conflicts to arise randomly. These random conflicts are resolved by social interaction accounting to the proponents of bourgeois political economy citizenship perspective. However, the theory failed to provide detailed analysis of the forces of social interaction and how these forces may lead to the disclosure of non-financial information by companies. In view of this it was decided to adopt more relevant organisational-based theories, namely legitimacy and stakeholder theories. The two theories were found to be the most relevant theories for analysing the relationship between organisations and different players within the external environments. The two theories were considered to be supplementing each other. Whilst legitimacy theory is of the view that companies provide sustainability information to justify their behaviours to society-at-large, the stakeholder theory provides information having taken the different stakeholders their informational needs into account. The author decided to apply these two theories jointly and inter-changeably due to their relationship.

CHAPTER 3

Sustainability reporting frameworks

3.1 Introduction

There are various guidelines, framework and recommendations which refer to sustainability disclosure. The following are some of the sustainability disclosure mechanisms or frameworks that are used in SR. This chapter is used to present Sustainability reporting frameworks such as International Organization for Standardization (ISO 26000 and ISO 14000), UN Compact, Principles of responsible investment initiarive, Performance Standards of International Finance Corporation (IFC), Performance Standards of International Finance Corporation (IFC), Policy on Social and Environmental Sustainability, Extractive Industries Transparency Initiative (EITI), Fundamental Principles for the Mining Sector (Berlin Guidelines), International Organization for Standardization (ISO 26000 and ISO 14000), AccountAbility 1000 (AA1000), Environmental Excellence in Exploration (E3), ICMM Principles for Sustainable Development and Voluntary Principles on Security and Human Rights Policy on Social and Environmental Sustainability. Finally the presentation of the Global Reporting Initiative Guidelines (GRI, version 3.0).

The important part of the choice of any of these framework is the extent of it transparency. Many companies are said to be using resources (time and money) on the preparation of sustainability reports in many varying volumes or pages. Some of the questions that may be asked are; what determine the size, level or volume of such report? Does it have any relationship with certain factors associated with the company's growth, size, performance or any other factors? These are simple but hard to answer questions since they require that a definition has been formulated on what sustainable development means for the organisation. Various recommendations and guidelines for SR have been published during recent years and following are some of them.

According to Lighteringen and Zadek, (2005) there are over 300 international standards and guidelines which are currently providing accepted reference standards for improving social and environmental performance and desired legitimacy, consistency and comparability which is required by business and its stakeholders. KPMG (2005) state that about 70% of social and environmental reports refer to the standards established under the UN system, including the Global Compact, ILO and the Declaration of Human Rights. These are followed by the OECD's Guidelines for Multinational Enterprises (11%). These facts go on to justify the use of the GRI in this study. There are a growing number of policy initiatives that, in the absence of effective mandatory rules, have aimed to establish high international standards for corporate behaviour. These vast numbers of principles, codes and frameworks have been formulated by civil society, international government organizations, and business advocacy groups, which emphasize the fundamentals of Corporate Social Responsibility. Assessing sustainability reporting various recommendations and guidelines for sustainability reporting have been published during recent years. A selection of international policy initiatives and codes of conduct is reviewed below.

3.2 International Standard ISO 26000:2010 (ISO 26000)

The International Standard ISO 26000:2010, Guidance on Social Responsibility, provides harmonized, globally relevant guidance for private and public sector organisations of all types based on international consensus among expert representatives of the main stakeholder groups, and so encourage the implementation of best practice in social responsibility worldwide. ISO 26000 is not specifically a sustainability disclosure framework, however as a guidance document it provides excellent information for organisations wishing to understand and address sustainability issues. It is closely aligned to the GRI framework and it strongly encourages sustainability disclosure by organisations. It is closely aligned to the GRI framework and it strongly encourages sustainability disclosure by organisation. The publication GRI and ISO 26000: How to use the GRI Guidelines in conjunction with ISO 26000 has more information on incorporating ISO 26000 into a GRI G3 or G3.1 based report.

3.3 UN Global Compact

The Global Compact is another voluntary initiative, which was launched by the United Nations on July 26, 2000. The UN Global Compact is committed to aligning their operations and strategies with ten (10) universally accepted principles in the areas of human rights, labour, environment and anti-corruption. These 10 principles offer a platform for corporate social responsibility which is entirely based on internationally agreed declarations. The participating companies of the UN Global Compact are required to issue an annual Communication on Progress (COP) to promote responsible corporate citizenship so that business can be part of the solution to the challenges of globalization and help to realize a more sustainable and inclusive global economy. In the context of a comprehensive CSR approach it can be seen as strength that GRI guidelines are compatible with the principles of the United Nation Global Compact. It must be stated here that these initiatives are not binding but rather rely on public accountability, transparency and the enlightened self-interest of companies, labour and civil society to employ and pursue these principles.

3.4 Principles for Responsible Investment Initiative (PRI)

The United Nations-backed Principles for Responsible Investment Initiative (PRI) is a network of international investors working together to put the six Principles for Responsible Investment into practice. The Principles were devised by the investment community. They reflect the view that environmental, social and corporate governance (ESG) issues can affect the performance of investment portfolios and therefore must be given appropriate consideration by investors if they are to fulfil their fiduciary (or equivalent) duty. The Principles provide a voluntary framework by which all investors can incorporate ESG issues into their decision-making and ownership practices &so better align their objectives with those of society at large.

3.5 Performance Standards of International Finance Corporation (IFC)

The Performance Standards, established by IFC in April 30, 2006 as one of the framework guiding the preparation of SR. It was designed to provide companies operating projects in emerging markets the capacity to manage their environmental and social risks. There are eight (8) performance standards involved and this has been shown in the Table 3.3 below. They contain stronger requirements for community engagement, biodiversity protection, community and worker grievance mechanisms, and the use of security forces, greenhouse gas emissions, and greater disclosure of public information by the IFC and client companies.

Table 3.1 IFC Performance Standard on
Environmental and Social Sustainability

Performance Standard 1:	Performance Standard 5:
Assessment and management of Environmental and Social risks and Impacts Underscores the importance of identifying EandS risks and impacts, and managing EandS performance throughout the life of a project.	**Land Acquisition and Involuntary resettlement** Applies to physical or economic displacement resulting from land transactions such as expropriation or negotiated settlements.
Performance Standard 2:	Performance Standard 6:
Labour and working conditions Recognizes that the pursuit of economic growth through employment creation and income generation should be balanced with protection of basic rights for workers.	**Biodiversity conservation and sustainable management of living natural resources** Promotes the protection of biodiversity and the sustainable management and use of natural resources.

Performance Standard 3:
Resource efficiency and pollution
Recognizes that increased industrial activity and urbanization often generate higher levels of air, water and land pollution, and that there are efficiency opportunities.

Performance Standard 4:
Community health, Safety and Security
Recognizes that projects can bring benefits to communities, but can also increase potential exposure to risks and impacts from incidents, structural failures, and hazardous materials.

Performance Standard 7:
Indigenous peoples
Aims to ensure that the development process fosters full respect for Indigenous Peoples.

Performance Standard 8:
Culture Heritage
Aims to protect cultural heritage from adverse impacts of project activities and support its preservation.

Source: www.ifc.org

3.6 Policy on Social and Environmental Sustainability

The Policy on Social and Environmental Sustainability provides specific details on the process used by IFC to assess risks and expected benefits of extractive industry projects (oil, gas and mining), including governance risks. The IFC seeks industry partners that share its vision and commitment to sustainable development, consistent with its own mission to carry out its investment and advisory services in ways that "do no harm" to people or the environment. The Policy on Social and Environmental Responsibility presents practical information to help resource and other companies enhance their competitive advantage through the adoption of socially and environmentally progressive policies and procedures.

3.7 Extractive Industries Transparency Initiative (EITI)

The Extractive Industries Transparency Initiative (EITI) is also one of the sustainability reporting initiative that guides the preparation of the report. It is a multi-stakeholder initiative, with partners from governments, NGOs, resource companies, investors, and industry and business associations. The EITI aims to ensure that revenues from extractive industries (oil, gas and mining) contribute to sustainable development and poverty reduction, as part of a broader goal to improve the social stability and investment climate of resource-rich nations. At the core of the EITI is a set of principles and criteria designed to strengthen transparency and accountability in transactions between governments and multinational companies. Currently, more than 20 nations are known to have committed to EITI principles and criteria since the initiative was launched in 2003. Ghana committed itself to participate in the Extractive Industries Transparency Initiative (EITI) at the International Conference in London on June 17, 2003 (SRC Consult, 2010).

3.8 Fundamental Principles for the Mining Sector (Berlin Guidelines)

The Fundamental Principles for the Mining Sector (Berlin Guidelines 1991, revised 2000) as an initiative guideline states that governments, mining companies and the minerals industries should as a minimum "Recognize the importance of socio-economic impact assessments and social planning in mining operations. The social-economic impacts should be taken into account at the earliest stages of project development being undertaken. Furthermore, gender issues should be considered at a policy and project level of the organisation. Recognize the linkages between ecology, socio-cultural conditions and human health and safety, the local community and the natural environment".

3.9 International Organization for Standardization (ISO 26000 and ISO 14000)

The International Organization for Standardisation (ISO) decided in 2004 to develop international standard guidelines for social responsibility (ISO 26000). It is intended for use by organizations of all types, in both public and private sectors, in developed and developing countries. The ISO is meant to assist them in their efforts to operate in the socially responsible manner that society increasingly demands. This would be analogous to its existing standards – for example ISO 14000 on environmental management. The ISO 14000 series is a collection of voluntary standards to help organizations meet the challenges of sustainable development. The standards provide both a model for streamlining environmental management and guidelines to ensure that environmental issues are considered within a decision-making framework.

3.10 AccountAbility 1000 (AA1000)

Another sustainability reporting guideline initiative is the AccountAbility 1000. It is a standard for social and ethical accounting, auditing and reporting. It aims to support companies by establishing indicators and objectives for their social impact, measuring progress and reporting. The involvement of the various interest groups is a central feature of AA1000. This initiative can be used to complement other reporting instruments (e.g. GRI), and can also be applied as a stand-alone system. AA1000 is process-oriented, in other words it gives no indications as to what content but focuses essentially on how to communicate. On the basis of AA1000, five modules are currently being prepared, each of which can be applied alone.

3.11 Environmental Excellence in Exploration (E3)

The Environmental Excellence in Exploration (E3) project is an electronic manual of good practices for companies in exploration activities. It has been built based on grassroots information proved by experts in the industry and seeks to give assistance to environmental management during the phase of exploration and implementation of rational practices of environmental management. The E3 project was conceived by a consortium of mining companies with the support of the Association of Mining Explorers and Promoters of Canada. In recent times, E3 has more than 1500 registered users in the world, including the mining sector, communities, governments, consultants, universities and NGOs among others.

3.12 ICMM Principles for Sustainable Development

The International Council for Minerals and Metals (ICMM) is sustainability guidelines initiatives made specifically for mineral and mining companies. In May 2003, ICMM an organization that reunites the main mining companies in the world, approved ten principles to promote sustainable development and committed its corporate members to measure their performance against these principles. The principles where extracted from the "Breaking New Ground" report from the Mining, Minerals and Sustainable Development Project (MMSD). The guidelines also include a commitment for public information, independently verified reporting and orientation about good management practices. The ICMM principles refer to corporate governance issues: corporate decision-making, human rights, risk management strategies, health and security, environment, biodiversity, integrated material management, community development and independent verification.

3.13 Voluntary Principles on Security and Human Rights

The Voluntary Principles on Security and Human Rights emanated from the dialogue between governments, companies and NGOs to serve as a guide in dealing with sustainable issues. They are basically promoted by the governments of the United States, the United Kingdom, Norway and the Netherlands, as well as companies from the extractives and energy sectors and to some extent non-governmental organizations like Oxfam. The Voluntary Principles comprise security and human rights issues and establish concrete lines of action to systematically evaluate and manage the risks and impacts of the corporate activity in these fields. The initiatives also offer guides for the relationship of corporations with State security organisms and private security companies, under a working framework that guarantees respect for Human Rights and the fundamental liberties in such organisations.

3.14 The Global Reporting Initiative Guidelines

Global Reporting Initiative (GRI), is one of the frameworks of SR which has assumed more popularity, most prominent and most widely adopted a number of companies preparing SR (e.g., Morhardt et al., 2002; Joseph, 2012), give meaning to the application of accounting to sustainability (Joseph, 2012). The framework came about as a result of the need for a consistent CSR reporting standard. GRI was founded in 1997 by the Coalition for Environmentally Responsible Economies (CERES) and the United Nations Environmental Programme (UNEP) and was initially published in 2000 (Isaksson and Steimle, 2009). The information guiding the preparation of SR can be obtained from the GRI website, particularly the "Sustainability Reporting Guidelines" Version 3.0 (or G3 Guidelines) and CorporateRegister.com. The GRI is a network-based organisation that pioneered the world's most widely used sustainability reporting framework. It is a long-term, multi-stakeholder, international process whose mission is to develop and disseminate globally applicable SR guidelines. GRI, as compare to other guidelines, provides detailed guidelines on "how to report," defining overall goal and content using principles and guidance, and "what to report" or determining content using standard disclosures and sector supplements (Joseph, 2012). The main focus of the analysis is on the key documented guidelines on concepts, measures and assurance, which was "developed through a unique multi-stakeholder consultative process involving representatives from reporting organizations and report information users from around the world" (GRI, 2010, p. 44).

The GRI (2010) defines SR as the practice of "measuring, disclosing, and being accountable to internal and external stakeholders for organizational performance towards the goal of sustainable development" (GRI, 2010, p. 3). This goal of sustainable development is used to mean, "Meeting the needs of the present without compromising the ability of future generations to meet their own needs." The GRI guidelines specifically have the main principle to achieve transparency. This transparency has been defined as the complete disclosure of information on the topics and indicators required to reflect impacts and enable stakeholders to make decisions (Joseph, 2012). The GRI concepts appeared to highlight transparency and sustainable development, with inter-generation equity forming the preferred theme underlying sustainability. However, GRI did not specify the contents of the report, but allowed for variations in the elements to comply with the initiatives. GRI also includes some general recommendations on what the report should contain, such as the extent to which the report preparer has applied the GRI Reporting Framework (including the Reporting Principles) in the course of reaching its conclusions. While the total firms reporting on sustainability and the nature of the reports continue to evolve, the statistics serve to provide an indication of the diversity of SR trends. Thus, GRI is representative of the SR, having a wide global application of firms from a variety of industries and of global (multi-national) nature.

GRI became independent in 2002, and published its second Sustainability Reporting Guidelines that year as the foundation upon which all other GRI reporting documents are based. The framework provides common guideline for sustainability reporting worldwide and is made to complement and strengthen financial reporting to shareholders. These guidelines are for voluntary use by organisations for reporting on the economic, environmental, and social dimensions of their activities, products, and services (GRI, 2010) to a broad and diverse range of stakeholders including the communities. The GRI aims to develop a globally applicable framework for an organisation's Sustainability and CSR reports. There are over 900 companies spread throughout 50 countries currently report on the basis of the GRI guidelines (Roca and Searcy, 2012).

The GRI is probably one of the most important initiatives as supplementary guidelines relevant to mining and metal sector has been developed to provide common framework guidelines for mining and metal companies. Their main purpose is to support companies in preparing SRs that integrate social, environmental and economic impacts of business on their stakeholders. The GRI is an internationally accepted framework that promotes comparable sustainability reporting (Isaksson and Steimle, 2009). The current version of the guidelines (GRI-G3) was published in 2010 which contains principles and guidance for defining content and quality of the sustainability report as well as for setting the report boundaries. In order to meet the continuous improvement and application worldwide GRI is currently in the process of developing G4, its fourth generation of sustainability reporting guidelines. An exposure draft of G4 was released for public consultation from 25 June to 25 September 2012 and can be still be accessed from the GRI webpage. GRI's core goals include the mainstreaming of disclosure on environmental, social and governance performance.

Many research has suggested that sustainable development indicators such as jobs, water usage, pollutant emissions, solid wastes, rehabilitation and land use, energy source and consumption, and health and safety are relevant for mining industry reporting (Byrne et al., 2002; Hilson and Basu, 2003; Azapagic, 2004; van Berkel and Bossilkov, 2004). The used of GRI framework by many companies was as a result of the many advantages associated with it; (1) the GRI framework is considered to have international acceptance; (2) has a rigorous framework for the application of triple bottom line reporting; (3) it was put together by a wide variety of experts after

Stakeholder consultation; (4) the GRI guidelines are easily accessible and (5) it is made to fit for all types of companies (Willis, 2003; Lamberton, 2005; Reynolds and Yuthas, 2008; Farneti and Guthrie, 2009). As its main purpose is to support companies in the preparation of SRs that integrate social, environmental and economic impacts of business, the GRI intends to establish guidelines that promote comparable SR (GRI, 2010). The framework contains principles and guidance for defining content and quality of the SR. It also has principles for setting the report boundaries, i.e. the determinants the parameters of the report.

There are three different types of disclosures which specify the base content that should appear in a SR according to the GRI guidelines. Companies should disclose three levels information types on their SR with respect to (1) Strategy and Profile disclosure (SPD), (2) Management Approach disclosures (MAD) and (3) Performance Indicators disclosures (PID) (see Figure 3.1 and Table 3.2).

Table 3.2 SR indicators in GRI guidelines

Strategy and Profile	Management Approach	Performance Indicators
1. Strategy and Analysis	1. Economic	EC1-EC9
2. Organisation Profile	2. Environmental	EN1-EN30
3. Report Parameters	3. Labour practice and decent Work	LA1-LA15
4. Governance, commitments and Engagement	4. Human Rights	HR1-HR11
	5. Society	SO1-SO10
	6. Product Responsibility	PR1-PR9

Source: *Adapted from GRI guidelines Version 3.0 (2006).*

3.14.1 Strategy and profile disclosures

The SPD consist of the main standard disclosure where the company's CEO has to provide an overall "strategy and analysis" that includes an overview of the strategy and risk factors (Joseph, 2012) see Table 3.3. The SPD set the overall context for understanding organizational performance such as its strategy, profile, and governance (GRI, 2010). It provides information on stated organisational aims or values and thus covers corporate recognition of the values of SR (e.g., striving for a reduction in energy consumption). The SPD provide a strategic view on the organisation's sustainability and the general level of the company's CSR activity. The regulations require the governance items be disclosed in a separate Section in the annual report. The areas to be disclosed in terms of this categories includes in broad areas Strategy and Analysis, Organisational Profile, Report Parameters and Governance, Commitments and Engagements which have been further been broken down in terms of items.

3.14.2 Management approach disclosure

The GRI guidelines provide a structured overview of the base content of MAD which are one of the disclosures in SR also cover how an organization addresses a given set of topics to provide context for understanding performance in a specific area such as economic, environmental, labour practices and decent work, human right, product responsibility and society (GRI, 2010; Bouten et al., 2011). It addresses a given CSR issue by describing the action or practice adopted. The MAD analyse the firm's approach in six areas of social interest and provide a context for understanding the performance in these areas. The MAD information types are referred to as areas and each of them has items/aspects to be disclosed (Robertson and Nicholson, 1996; Vuontisjärvi, 2006; Bouten et al., 2011). In addition to MAD three categories of indicators, i.e., economic, social, and environmental, the GRI also specifically provides "sector guidance supplements" for use by different industries to address the unique issues in that industry (Joseph, 2012). These sector supplements guides sectors such as Financial Services, Metals, Telecommunications, Public Service and others (Joseph, 2012). It is expected that GRI continues to develop and update sector supplements from time to time to make them relevant to those industries.

3.14.3 Performance Indicators

The PIs are developed to provide more detail in each of the six management approach disclosure (MAD) areas while the sector supplements provide the measures, along with indicators that are specific to the industry (Joseph, 2012; GRI, 2010). The sustainability PIs are organized by economic, environmental, and social categories. Social Indicators are further categorized by Labour, Human Rights, Society, and Product Responsibility. PIs elicit comparable information on MAD performance of the organization and CSR achievements by providing quantitative measures of CSR performance (GRI. 2010). There are two categories of PI that should be disclosed namely set of Core and Additional Performance Indicators. Core Indicators are intended to identify generally applicable Indicators and are assumed to be material for most organizations which they are expected to report on unless they are deemed immaterial based on GRI Reporting Principles. According to the G3 guidelines, core indicators are developed through the multi-stakeholder process and are assumed to apply to all firms (Joseph, 2012). Additional Indicators also address the emerging topics that may be material for some organizations, but are not material for others. For example where Sector Supplements exist, the Indicators should be treated as Core Indicators (GRI, 2010). Reporting organizations are encouraged to follow this structure in preparing their SRs, however, other formats may be chosen.

The GRI aims to achieve uniform and consistent reporting on sustainability performance, allowing this to be as routine and comparable as financial reporting (Isaksson and Steimle, 2009). But GRI like any initiative have some strengths and weaknesses. One of such strengths has been the fact that it has a multi-stakeholder features in the process of SR preparation (Brown et al., 2009a). Furthermore, Brown et al. (2009a) argue that the GRI have many characteristics of an established institution, including widespread uptake, legitimacy, emergence of new business activities, and emergence of competitive pressures related to the GRI, among others. The GRI has also been criticized on many occasions such as, confusion over its scope, the lack of a requirement for independent verification of the report, and the fact that different levels of application permit selective reporting on the performance indicators (Moneva et al., 2006; Roca and Searcy, 2012).

3.15 Conclusion

This Chapter presented reviewed existing empirical literature on sustainability reporting frameworks. It also reviewed the type of information of the GRI such as Strategy and Profile disclosures, Management approach and performance indicators respectively. The information categories included in each group were subsequently presented and, where appropriate the relevant literature is reviewed and discussed to explain why each category was considered.

CHAPTER 4

Content analysis in the sustainability reporting research

4.1 Introduction

This Chapter seeks to look at the empirical analysis of the research questions which aims to investigate the effects of corporate characteristics of the mining companies in Ghana on the level of disclosure in the sustainability reports (SR). Investigation is made by a collection of empirical evidence on research questions as presented in Chapter 3 which are focused on examining the significance of the relationships between corporate characteristics such as size, growth rate, profitability ratio, gearing rate, efficiency ratio, working capital ratio, age and complexity of the MCGs and the level of SR. Each of the research questions is investigated using the relevant techniques that were discussed earlier.

The level of SR is defined here as the extent or volume of sustainability information covered in the SR in terms of words, pages and paragraphs. It will be interesting to know the determinants of the level of information in SR. Though it was argued that companies disclose sustainability information to justify their actions but what actually determine the level has not been extensively researched. The chapter presents the analysis of the determinants of the level of SR comprises of descriptive statistics, the correlation analysis results, and regression results of size of the MCG and the level of SR, the growth rates and the SR level of the company, the Profitability of the MCG and the level of SR, the Efficiency of the MCGs and the level of SR, the Capital gearing ratio of the MCG and the level of SR, the working capital of the MCG and the level of SR, the age of the MCG and the level of SR and the complexity of the MCG and the level of SR. The overall findings of these eight supporting research questions are summed up in the conclusion and summary.

Many studies have concluded that there has been a rise in the level of SR in recent times (Gray et al., 2001). In the literature attempt has been made to explore the relationships between social and environmental disclosures and corporate characteristics (Ullmann, 1985; Mathews, 1987; Gray et al., 1995a; Gray et al., 2001) such as size, growth, profitability, efficiency, capital gearing, working capital, age and complexity of the MCGs to examine whether any relationship exists between them. This means that this study will be one of the first to compare the level of SR and the corporate characteristics. As it is in most countries, companies in Ghana are also under no regulatory requirements to prepare SR, hence, only few companies prepare SR. Using theoretical explanation above it was argued that in the context of stakeholder and legitimacy theories, in the absence of any regulatory or obligatory requirements companies are likely to prepare SR for legitimacy purposes by adopting the strategies 2, 3 and 4 of Lindblom (2010). For instance, MCGs may use information relating to Lindblom's Strategy 2 - to change the perception of their relevant public without having to change their actual behaviours, or Strategy 3 - to manipulate that perception, deflecting attention from issues of concern to other related issues, and/or (4) change external expectations of its performance.

The dependent variable in this study is the level of sustainability report, otherwise known as environmental disclosure, or CSR disclosure, as it is used in many studies. Measurement techniques used in previous studies of SR can be categorized into two groups: the ones that count disclosures, and the ones that classify them (Milne and Adler, 1999; Burgwal and Vierira, 2014). The first group uses measures that quantify the level of environmental disclosure e.g. number of pages, sentences and words, or number of disclosure items (Deegan and Gordon, 1996; Gray et al., 1995; Guthrie and Parker, 1989; Hackston and Milne, 1996; Milne and Adler, 1999; Neu et al., 1998; Patten, 2002). The level of a sustainability report is measured by these three variables namely number of words, pages and paragraphs (e.g., Hackston and Milne, 1996; Gray et al., 2001; Patten, 2002; Bouten et al., 2012) which will be discussed in detail in subsequently. The main criticism on this type of measurement is that non-textual information is not taken into account (McMurtrie, 2005) and it is impossible also to assess the quality of the disclosed information (Burgwal and Vierira, 2014).

Table 4.1 Dependent and Independent Variables

Variables	Description	Measurement	Role in model
LWD	Log of Words	Number of words in SR	Dependent
LPAG	Log of Pages	Number of pages in SR	Dependent
LPAR	Log of Paragraphs	Number of paragraphs in SR	Dependent
LSZ	Log of Size	Size of company based on Revenue	Independent
LGRO	Log of Growth	Change in asset and R&D	Independent
LPRO	Log of Profitability	Return on Equity ratio	Independent
LEFF	Log of Efficiency	Asset Turnover ratio	Independent
LGEA	Log of Gearing	Debt-equity ratio	Independent
LAG	Log of Age	Number of years in operation	Independent
LWC	Log of Working Capital	Current asset ratio	Independent
LCOM	Log of Complexity	Number of subsidiaries	Independent

Source: Author

The increase in environmental awareness has led to a growing demand for environmental accountability by organizations. Therefore preparing sustainability report is a medium used to explain CSR policies and to take responsibilities for ethical, social and environmental actions (Adams, 2004; Brammer and Pavelin, 2006; Burgwal and Vierira, 2014). Since the mid-1990s, attention for environmental accounting related research has been increased with the majority of research relating to the corporate and the country specific determinants of environmental disclosure (see examples, Bartiaux, 2008; Bassetto, 2010; Beck, Campbell and Shrives, 2010; Christ and Burritt, 2013; Clarkson et al., 2011; Cormier and Magnan, 2003; Deegan and Gordon, 1996; Dong, Ishikawa et al., 2011; Erlandsson and Tillman, 2009; Hackston and Milne, 1996; Harte and Owen, 1991; Kolk and Perego, 2010; Murray et al., 2006; Roberts, 1992; Rosa, 2012; Silva Monteiro and Aibar-Guzmán, 2010; Tilt and Symes, 1999; Trierweiller et al., 2012; Burgwal and Vieira, 2014).

Table 4.2 Independent Variables Measurement and Justification

Independent variables	Measurement	Justification/References
Size	Natural logarithm of Revenue	Lu and Abeysekera (2014); Clarkson et al. (2008); Hackston and Milne, (1996); Trotman and Bradley, (1981); Hahn and Kuhnen (2013); Fortune 500 Ayadi, (2007); Belkaoui and Karpik, (1989); Patten, (1991); Roberts, (1992); Gray et al. (2001); Joseph and Taplin, (2011); Fortanier et al., (2011); Gallo and Jones Christensen, (2011).
Growth	Change in assets and R&D	Padgett and Galan (2010); Lourenço and Branco, (2013); Artiach et al., (2010).
Profitability	Return on Equity ratio	Parsa and Kouhy, (2001); Lourenco and Branco, (2013); Cowen et al., (1987); Hackston and Milne, (1996); Burgwal and Viera, (2014); Uadiale and Fagbemi, (2012); Bouten et al., (2012); Hossain and Hammami (2009).

Gearing	Debt-equity ratio	Lourenco and Branco (2013); Burgwal and Viera, (2014); Parsa and Kouhy, (2001); Artiach et al., 2010); Ziegler and Schröder, (2010); Lu and Abeysekera (2014).
Managerial efficiency	Asset Turnover ratio	Waddock et al. (1997); Bouten et al., (2012); Parsa and Kouhy, (2001) Lu and Abeysekera (2014).
Working Capital	Current asset ratio	Waddock *et al.* (1997); Parsa and Kouhy, (2001)
Age	Number of years in operation	Singh and Ahuja, (1983); Hossain and Hammami (2009); Akhtaruddin (2005), Haniffa and Cooke (2002), Glaum and Street (2003); Hossain (2008)
Complexity	Number of subsidiaries	Hossain and Hammami (2009); Haniffa, and Cooke, (2002); Owusu-Ansah, S. (1998); Lu and Abeysekera (2014).

Source: Author

The independent variables in this study are corporate characteristics such as corporate size, growth, profitability, gearing, working capital, efficiency, age, and complexity. These were arrived at after extensive review of prior research to explore the relationships between corporate/industry characteristics and the level of social/environmental reporting or sustainability reports (see for example, Cowen et al., 1987; Roberts, 1992; Gray et al., 2001; Cormier and Magnan, 2003; Al-Tuwaijri et al., 2004; Cormier et al., 2005; Aerts and Cormier, 2009; Bouten et al., 2012; Burgwal and Vieira, 2014). With reference to the research objectives the variables used in the study are given in Table 4.2. There have been many studies which have examined the level of sustainability reporting in relation to corporate characteristics. As noted above, the next stage is to examine if there is any relationship between SR and these characteristics with the use of the following number of research questions posed for the investigation of the study.

The data from annual reports were collected for more than one year in order to provide greater confidence in the results. One of the determining factors for choosing the years is to use the most recent data as possible. Another factor that was taken into account in the selection of these years is the availability of data regarding the level of SR practices in the Ghana. The main empirical examines the determinants of the levels of SR. To examine determinants of SR, MCGs were chosen, as they provide a high level of SR and consequently more confidence in the results can be anticipated. Therefore, it can be argued that the results from such a sample are more general. In this study, the relationships were investigated by initially computing the degree of relationships between the variables using simple correlations coefficient analysis and the effects of the independent variables on dependent was analysed in a multiple linear regression model to investigate the research objective. Whilst the correlation analysis focuses on the strength of the relationship between two or more variables, regression analysis assumes a dependence or causal relationship between one or more independent and dependent variables.

It can be argued that the level of SR or how much information a MCGs discloses on its SR may depend on certain characteristics and factors associated with the company. These factors which may affect the level of SR are corporate characteristics as depicted in the Figure 4.2. Size as one of the factors may have some effect on the level of disclosure in the SR to the extent that large sized companies with high degree of activities may have the broader society's attention and consequently face the highest degree of social scrutiny and more pressure for communication its activities. According to legitimacy theory, these companies need to legitimise their activities to a greater extent by having a positive or good relationship between them and the society in which they find themselves. In view of this characteristic of a company, this may have an effect on the level of SR they prepare.

4.3 Content analysis procedures

Content analysis is a technique whereby text is codified into groups or categories according to specific criteria (Milne and Adler, 1999). It has been defined by Krippendorff (1980, p. 21) as: "a research technique for making replicable and valid inferences from data according to their context." Using content analysis (CA) in this study, qualitative information from the Annual reports (AR) was converted to quantitative measures by counting the number words, paragraphs and pages. These are considered measures of the level of sustainability report as used in other studies such as Deegan and Rankin, (1996) and Wilmshurst and Frost, (2000) where words counts were used, Milne and Adler (1999), Deegan et al. (2000) where paragraphs counts were used and Gray et al. (1995) and Campbell (2000) where pages counts were employed. Words count is a robust measure level of SR in which counting errors are less likely than other measurements (Campbell et al., 2003). Paragraphs count and page proportions count have similar advantages, although as compared to word count, page count may produce a more diluted result whilst a paragraph with longer or shorter length might present different levels of quality of information just as with page count (Campbell et al., 2003).

The level of disclosure in SR is measured using a volumetric word count because disclosures can be assessed qualitatively, as suggested by Hackston and Milne (1996). In this study all three counts were used with the justification that other researchers have also used them (word, page and paragraph count methods) as they are capable of generating volumetric measures of disclosure (Campbell, 2004). Furthermore, the method has been employed widely in western countries (Hackstone and Milne, 1996; Milne and Adler, 1999; Guthrie et al., 2008) and Asian countries (Thompson and Zakaria, 2004; Xiao et al., 2005; Ratanajongkol et al., 2006). For example, word counts are seen to be an appropriate reflection of the importance that companies attach to level of SR (Campbell et al., 2006; Gray et al., 1995a; Ratanajongkol et al., 2006; Wilmshurst and Frost, 2000) and have been found to be highly correlated to other measures, such as sentences or percentage of pages (Islam and Deegan, 2008, p. 859). After extracting SR quantitative information from the sample of the MCGs' AR for 2008 to 2012, the data was analysed. There has been no previous content analysis where all the three measurements (in terms of word, paragraph or page count) of the SR disclosure levels in annual reports in Ghana have been adopted and the current study attempts to bridge this gap and as far as I know this is a fact.

The study, using CA, measures both the presence/absence of items (e.g. Cormier et al., 2005; Branco and Rodrigues, 2008; Jose and Lee, 2007; Bouten et al., 2011), and the extent of the disclosures on those items (e.g. Unerman, 2000; Gray et al., 2001; Campbell, 2004). A coding structure helps in reducing decision schemes where large numbers of alternatives are involved, and when recording involves several dimensions of judgment (Krippendorff, 2004; Bouten et al., 2011). Decision schemes offer coders the opportunity to determine each one separately (Krippendorff, 2004).

All the annual reports used in the study were collected from the official website of the MCGs in PDF format. Where it is not available, demand was made directly to the company for it. As PDF files do not contain a word count function the PDF files were converted to Microsoft Word files for text analysis. During conversion the some graphics were lost, so graphic analysis was excluded, but the procedure ensured that all reports were adjusted to a unified page and paragraph format (McMurtrie, 2005). This was followed by the cleaning-up of the irrelevant and inaccurately transcribed items which include some components of the text, such as pictures, footnotes, page and Section headings, page numbers, charts/graphs and signatures. These were deleted from the texts because a decision was taken not to include some components of the text. The reason is that they do not contain the unit of analyses which this study has chosen to analyse. After the cleaning, the texts were put into the Oxford Concordance Programme (OCP) to find the frequency distributions of the number of words, pages and paragraphs appearing in them, a process adopted in Borkowski et al. (2012).

Finally, the literature was reviewed, which resulted in the determination of keywords represented and identified the sustainability issues. In the analysis the MCGs characteristics such as size, growth rate, profitability, efficiency, working capital ratio, age and complexity were used to find out their effects on the level of the SR. The overall aim of the study is to fill the gap in the existing knowledge by assessing the sustainability reporting practices of MCGs in the absence of any regulatory requirements. It is believed that companies in general and MCGs in particular are unlikely to freely provide adequate information to meet informational requirements of their stakeholders and even if they do the extent may vary across companies depending on the characteristics of such companies.

4.4 Units of measurement

There are different units of measurement and it is important that an appropriate unit is selected and how such system can be reliable. One of the main assumptions underlying content analysis is that the volume of disclosure reflects the kind of importance preparers of the report attach to a particular issue (Gray et al. 1995b; Neu et al., 1998; Unerman, 2000; Krippendorff, 2004; Beattie and Thomson, 2007; Striukova et al., 2008; Bouten et al., 2012). The methods used in previous research has frequently measured the extent of reporting by counting the number of words, sentences and pages to quantify disclosure (e.g., Hackston and Milne, 1996; Gray et al., 2001; Patten, 2002; Bouten et al., 2012). Previous studies suggest that these types of measurement (i.e. number of words, sentences, pages or page proportion) have both advantages and disadvantages (see Unerman, 2000). However, both 'word' and 'paragraph' have the disadvantage of ignoring non-narrative CSR disclosure (i.e. photographs and figures) and thus lower the total amount of disclosure (Unerman, 2000).

A disclosure index is another method which has also been frequently used to capture the number of items a company reports on (e.g. Cowen et al., 1987; Belkaoui and Karpik, 1989; Patten, 2002; Ho and Taylor, 2007; Branco and Rodrigues, 2008; Clarkson et al., 2008). It is also referred to as incidence rate (see Milne and Adler, 1999; Bouten et al., 2012). A disclosure index measuring the number of items is thus informed by slightly different considerations than a word, sentence or page count. The main shortcoming of measuring the disclosure level by looking at the extent of the disclosures, or by counting the number of disclosed items, is that general and specific disclosures are treated in the same way (see Al-Tuwaijri et al., 2004; Cormier et al., 2005; Aerts et al., 2008). The following are the measurements used in this study.

The measurement of level of SR in terms of words was justified by maintaining that level of disclosure can thereby be recorded in greater detail (Deegan and Gordon, 1996; Mahadeo et al., 2011). According to Zeghal and Ahmed (1990), words are the smallest unit of measurement and can be expected to provide the maximum strength to the study in assessment of the level of SR. The amount of disclosure (per theme and per company) is measured using a volumetric word count. Word counts are seen to be an appropriate reflection of the importance that companies attach to the level of SR (Campbell et al., 2006; Gray et al., 1995a; Ratanajongkol et al., 2006; Wilmshurst and Frost, 2000; Mahadeo et al., 2011) and have been found to be highly correlated to other measures, such as sentences or percentage of pages (Islam and Deegan, 2008, p. 859). One of the criticism of using words as a basis for measurement is that, it is considered to be ambiguous measure, leaves the researchers pondering which individual word is SR and which is not, therefore, the possibility remains that disagreement between different coders could be quite serious (Hackston and Milne, 1996, p.84). Furthermore, Milne and Adler, (1999) argued that individual word alone cannot provide a sound basis for SR without a sentence or sentences for context. Word as a unit of measurement has the advantage of giving a detailed description of SR with more accuracy (Zeghal and Ahmed, 1990).

The measurement of the level of SR in terms of paragraph was justified in the sense that paragraph can be counted with more accuracy than words according to Hackston and Milne (1996). The use of paragraph to measure the level of SR also helps to convey meaning whereas discerning the meaning of individual words in isolation is problematic (Hackston and Milne, 1996, p.84). Using paragraphs as a unit of measurement seems to ignore that the differences in use of grammar may result in conveying the same message by using a similar number of words (Unerman, 2000, p.675). A strong criticism raised against measuring the level of SR in terms of number of words or paragraphs by Unerman (2000) is that the results ignore non-narrative disclosure such as photographs or charts which has been known to be an effective methods of communication (Unerman, 2000, p.675). Ignoring photographs (which are sometimes more powerful tool than narrative disclosure) have the effect of preventing those who does not have either time or inclination to read every word in the ARs (Unerman, 2000, p.675).

The study also measures the level of SR in terms of number of pages, in addition to number of words and paragraphs. The main reason of using three different measurement units is that the results will help reveal whether using them can provide similar results or not. One of the main criticisms of using number of pages to measure the level of SR is that print sizes, column sizes, and pages sizes may differ from AR to another (Ng, 1985). Therefore, Newson and Deegan (2002) measured the SR to the nearest hundredth of a page. Recognising the advantage of the 'page' method suggested by these studies, the present study uses the method to measure the level of SR. A summary of the most commonly used units is shown in Table 4.3.

Table 4.3 The Coding Units

Coding Unit	Meaning/Example
Words/phrases/terms	According to Hussey and Hussey (1996), words/phrases/terms can be used to examine minutes of company/union meetings (disputes) or to examine circulars to shareholders for the words (increased dividends).
Paragraph	Paragraph as a measure of "... is infrequently used ... because of its complexity. Coders have the difficulty in classifying and coding the numerous and varied elements covered in a single paragraph" (Nachmias and Nachmias, 1996, p.327).
Theme	A theme is a simple sentence which has a subject and a predicate (Nachmias and Nachmias, 1996). For instance, in examining either the minutes of meetings on occasions where discussions lead to agreements or trying send AR to shareholders where increases in productivity are linked to increased profits (Hussey and Hussey 1996).
Character	When the recording unit is a character, "the researcher counts the number of persons appearing in the test rather than the number of words or themes" (Nachmias and Nachmias, 1996, p.327).

Source: Author

4.5 Validity and reliability

There are two main types of validity that need to be established in a research project, viz content validity and results validity (see Saunders et al., 2007). Whilst content validity refers to the extent to which the content analysis method measures what it intends to measure, results validity concerns "the extent to which results are really about that they profess to be about" (Saunders et al., 2007, p. 614). Krippendorff (2004, pp. 313-338) describes a variety of procedures that are used to establish the content and results validity in content analysis. For the purpose of establishing content validity, and because of time constraints, this research used a semantic validity procedure to ensure that the features selected for investigation accurately describe meanings in the context of this research (Krippendorff, 2004); that is, that the features could be easily identifiable by experts in the field of sustainability reporting as characteristic of the practice. Hence, the features were drawn from an extensive review of the literature on sustainability reporting, with particular focus on the United Kingdom case, and were then approved by an expert in the field. Thus, the features seemed reasonable (see Robson, 2002). Moreover, results validity was established by the predictive validity procedure (Krippendorff, 2004). In other words, based on the review of the literature on sustainability reporting possible answers were envisaged with regard to the trends of the features selected for investigation. Hence, observations in the dataset validate the predictions made.

The term reliability refers to "the extent to which the data collection method will yield consistent findings" (Saunders et al. 2007, p. 609). According to Milne and Adler (1999) CA classification must be reliable in terms of consistency and reproducibility. These are ensured by using specific decision rules in categorisation, sub-categorisation and measurement processes. The existence of reliability ensures the same results when applied at a different time, thus ensuring reliability and reproducibility (Gray et al., 1995b). For example, Milne and Adler (1999) empirically tested the reliability and validity of CA by using different people who measure and code and the result showed that the method is valid and reliable in capturing the level of total SR

The basic characteristic of CA is that the data should be tested to prove that they are objective, systematic and reliable (Krippendorff, 1980). As Hayes and Krippendorff (2007) state, "conclusions from such data can be trusted only after demonstrating their reliability" (Hayes and Krippendorff, 2007, p.77). The reliability of measurement is measured using the inter-coder test in which the disclosure is assessed by the researcher and another person, and the results then compared. The ARs were reviewed by both a researcher and another person. Then the inter coder reliability was measured using a number of reliability measures. The differences in the results were discussed to identify the reasons for these differences. There are different measures or indices of inter-coder reliability, and there is no theoretical basis for choosing between them. Hayes and Krippendorff (2007) suggest that a good measure of reliability should have the following properties:

- It should assess the agreement between two or more coders;
- It should be grounded in the distribution of the categories or scale points actually used by the coders;
- It should constitute a numerical scale between at least two points with sensible reliability interpretations;
- It should be appropriate to the level of measurement of the data; and
- Its sampling behaviour should be known or at least computable.

Neuendorf (2002, p.141) states that "when human coders are used in CA, this translates to inter-coder reliability or level of agreement among two or more coders". Neuendorf (2002, p.146) notes that in CA, reliability should be assessed at two points, pilot and final. In this study, a pilot test was conducted on a random sample of 20% of the total sample of the ARs in order to verify the performance of the coding form. The data collected were reviewed by an academic researcher who in his role as expert in the field of SR confirmed the results. Next, during the data gathering processing a final reliability test was conducted by two different coders (the researcher and a PhD student who received training on the subject) in order to verify the performance/consistency of the researcher in collecting the data. A random sample of 20% of the total number of statements was selected to conduct this final reliability test.

Firstly, inter-coder reliability was measured (for the number of words, number of pages and number of paragraphs) and the examination of the validity of disclosure measurement categories or classification of SR index otherwise known as management approach (economic, environmental, human right, labour practices and decent work, product responsibility and society) were examined for internal consistency with the use of Cronbach's coefficient alpha of reliability. The Cronbach's coefficient alpha should have a minimum value of 0 and a maximum value of 1, and normally when the alpha value is 0.7 or more this is considered as an acceptable value for reliability (Botosan, 1997; Gul and Leung, 2004). The Cronbach's coefficient alpha of reliability for the six types in the disclosure index are 0.98, 0.99, 0.99, 0.98 and 0.94 in 2008, 2009, 2010, 2011 and 2012 respectively. The results indicate that there is internal consistency among the sustainability information types in the SR.

4.6 Descriptive statistics

Descriptive statistics for the $\log_e$ data employed in the analysis are shown in Table 4.4. The mean, standard deviation, minimum and maximum values for (a) the three types of measurement of SR and (b) all eight company characteristics are provided. Measures of skewness and kurtosis are also given. Descriptive statistics for the dependent and independent variables are presented in Table 4.4 indicates the level of SR in terms of words, pages and paragraphs. The skewness and kurtosis figures are, in most cases, low indicating that the distributions of the (transformed) disclosure variables are normal. Two notable exceptions are Profitability ratio and gearing ratio which are negatively skewed; for each of these variables there is a small number of companies which disclose relatively large amounts of this type of information. The minimum number of words in the report was 9.57 and a maximum of 12.02 with a mean of about 10.80. These results also reflect that SR increases with respect to words and pages within the same period as compared with the study of Hackston and Milne (1996). The number of pages has the minimum of 3.85 and maximum of 5.97 with a mean of 4.72. This increase in average number of pages is also consistence with many previous studies (for example Cowen, et al., 1987; Patten, 1991; Hackston and Milne, 1996), and this reflects the increasing interest in corporate sustainability disclosures. The number of paragraphs having a minimum of 5.08 and a maximum of 10.01 has a mean of 8.36.

These results show that minimum disclosure in words, pages and paragraphs as reported indicate that all MCGs did prepare SR to some extent. This high interest in the preparation of SR reflect, as expected, the growing interest of MCGs in the preparation of SR and justify the consistency with earlier study of Guthrie and Parker (1990) that more companies are disclosing more sustainability information. According to Andrew et al. (1989) developing countries indicate lower percentages in the preparation of SR, for example, only 26% of 119 publicly-listed companies in Malaysia and Singapore, disclose sustainability information. In Table 4.5, it is also observed that the size ranged from 4.68 minimum to 9.25, maximum words with a mean of 7.14. The utilisation of natural logarithm of size in the regression analysis mitigated the skewness to -0.12 and this is consistent with studies made by Glaum and Street (2003). It can also be seen from the Table 4.4 that growth rate from a minimum of 1.39 to maximum of 3.70 with a mean of 2.66. The growth rate distribution also showed some skewness (-0.15) but this was mitigated by utilizing natural logarithm of growth rate in the regression analysis (Glaum and Street, 2003).

Table 4.4 Descriptive statistics

Variables	Obs.	Median	Mean	SD.	Min.	Max.	Skew.	Kurt.
LWD	50	10.62	10.80	0.70	9.57	12.02	0.25	1.86
LPAG	50	4.62	4.72	0.62	3.85	5.97	0.24	1.75
LPAR	50	8.37	8.36	1.03	5.08	10.01	-1.06	5.19
LSZ	50	7.10	7.14	1.45	4.68	9.25	-0.12	1.49
LGRO	50	4.31	2.66	0.63	1.39	3.70	-0.15	2.10
LPRO	50	4.95	4.71	1.08	-1.61	5.13	-4.95	27.48
LEFF	50	1.47	1.11	1.25	-2.53	2.34	-1.87	5.45
LGEA	50	6.21	6.17	0.47	2.94	6.51	-6.43	44.33
LWC	50	0.72	0.94	1.23	-1.31	3.97	1.10	3.90
LAG	50	2.80	2.88	0.84	1.79	4.50	0.63	2.47
LCOM	50	1.95	1.82	0.41	1.10	2.40	-0.37	1.84

Sources: Author

Notes:

1. Descriptive statistics for the transformed (natural log) variables employed in the analysis and those for the corporate characteristics used as explanatory variables are shown in Table.
2. SD is the standard deviation, Obs., Min. and Max. denote number of observation, minimum and the maximum, Skew. and Kurt. denote the coefficients of skewness and kurtosis respectively.
3. LWD, LPAG and LPAT stand for natural log words, pages and paragraphs respectively. LSZ, LGRO, LPRO, LEFF, LGEA, LWC, LAG and LCOM denote natural log of size, growth, profitability, efficiency, working capital, age and complexity.

From Table 4.4 on descriptive analysis the profitability ratio have a minimum of -1.61 to a maximum of 5.13 with a mean of 4.71. This implies that more profitable MCGs do not disclose significantly more sustainability information than do less profitable ones. The result is thus inconsistent with some previous studies such as Singhvi and Desai (1971) and Hossain and Reaz (2007), however, other studies show positive influence such as Ghazali and Weetman (2006) and Al-Shammari (2008). Moreover, to date, the empirical evidence on the relationship between the performance of a company and disclosure is mixed (Lang and Lundholm, 1993; Wallace et al., 1994; Camfferman and Cooke, 2002). One possible answer for the insignificance of the variable is that apparently merges and acquisitions of some of the companies within the last decade.

The efficiency measures how management effectively manage the organisation. Asset turnover ratio is used to measure the efficiency of management. The efficiency ratio according to Table 4.4 ranged from -2.53 minimum to 2.34 maximum with a mean of 1.11. It indicates that MCGs have low fixed assets against total turnover. The age of the MCGs ranges from 1.79 minimum to 4.20 maximum with a mean of 2.88 for the sample. The age as a variable is expected to be positive and significant which suggests that older companies will produce more sustainability information on SR. The table also presented that complexity has a minimum of 1.10 and the maximum being 2.40. The mean of complexity variable is shown as 1.82 according to the Table. These figures indicate that there is no MCG without a subsidiary. The companies in general are reluctant to disclose information unobligated considering the cost of preparing those information.

4.7 Correlation analysis

Before empirical analysis of data, it is essential to look at the degree of relationships between these measurements and variables. Table 4.5 shows the correlation matrix between the dependent and independent variables of the study for all the period under study. Here the results are largely consistent with previous literature. The level of SR is measured by the number of words, pages, and paragraphs. In the first instance, multicollinearity assumption is tested with the use of a correlation matrix among the variables. As discussed above, the skewness and kurtosis statistics reported in Table 4.4 suggested that the variables generally suffer from mild non-normal behaviour. In view of this, Spearman's non-parametric correlation coefficients are presented in Table 4.5 to throw more light on the issue of normality.

It can be seen from Table 4.5 that the coefficients of the non-parametric correlations may be mild, and this is consistent with those reported by prior studies (Haniffa and Hudaib, 2006, p. 1048, 1050-1051; Cheung and Wei, 2006, p.913; Francoeur et al., 2008, p.88). By contrast, Table 4.5 shows that there are high and moderate correlations between the dependent variables, namely number of words, paragraphs and pages which are expected since they are proxies of the same measure, level of SR report. As expected these high and moderate correlations are statistically tolerable among these dependent variables and this appears to suggest that it may be a relevant instrument. The highest correlation value is 0.92 is between number of words and pages, followed by number of words and paragraphs (r = 0.60) and pages and paragraphs (r = 0.52) which are moderate. These high values are a normal result for variables measuring the same index.

During the period under consideration, the degree of relationship between the level of SR and MCGs' size in order are: r = 0.69 with p-value < 0.00 for words, r = 0.66 with p-value < 0.00 for pages and r = 0.40 with p-value < 0.00 with respect to paragraph. These indicate moderate and very highly significant relationship. Therefore, the level of SR is significantly correlates positively with size of the MCGs. As corporate size appears to be highly correlated with SR, the result is consistent with that of Hackston and Milne (1996) who asserted that size is highly correlated with the amount of social disclosure. It is also in line and consistent with Parsa and Kouhy (2008), who also found a significant correlation between two measures of size and social disclosure. Table 4.5 shows the relation between the number of words and the size (LSZ) of the MCG was noted to be slightly higher as compared with paragraphs and pages which show similar correlation with the level of SR.

The growth rate shows very low correlation with the level of SR in terms of words, pages and paragraphs (r = 0.09 with p-value = 0.52, r = -0.08 with p-value = 0.56 and r = -0.17 with p-value = 0.23 respectively). In Table 4.5, all of the three dependent variables do not have any significant relationship with growth rate (GRO) and number of words and pages having a positive coefficient. This means the growth rate appears to be less correlated with the level of SR and do not have any significant relationship. According to the results, profitability (LPRO) and the level of SR also have some correlation with the dependent variables (r = 0.22 for words with p-value = 0.13, r = 0.22 for pages with p-value = 0.11 and r = -0.01 with p-value = 0.95 for paragraphs. There is a weak or negative correlation between LPRO and paragraphs (LPAR).

With regards to the efficiency (LEFF) of the MCGs and the level of SR, the results show a positive correlation with the level SR. The efficiency of the management showed a positive relationship with disclosure level in

SR but a weak degree of correlation (r = 0.35 for words, r = 0.17 for pages and r = 0.18 for paragraphs) with insignificant p-values. The corporate efficiency variables results tend to be consistent over the period and indicate significant correlation with the level of SR. These results show that the level of SR is correlated with extent of efficiency of the MCG.

The level of SR showed a positive relationship with capital gearing ratio (LGEA) though with a low degree of correlation. The values of correlation are: r=0.13 with p-value = 0.36 for words, r= 0.05 with p-value = 0.73 for pages and r= 0.06 with p-value = 0.70 for paragraphs. The results from the corporate gearing ratio variable appear to be positively correlated with the level of SR in terms of all the measurements but insignificant. The positive correlation between gearing and the level of SR indicates that the greater dispersion of the type of ownership is related to a higher level of disclosure in the SR though insignificant. During the period of this study, the degree of the relationship between working capital ratio (LWC) ratio and the level of SR is highly significant for all SR measurements as it can be seen that the various p-values are less than 0.05. It can also be seen from Table 4.6 that the correlations coefficients and p-values are: r = -0.50 with p-value = 0.00 for words, r = -0.41 with p-value = 0.00 for pages and r=-0.30 with p-value = 0.03 for paragraphs. Therefore, LWC is negatively significantly correlated with SR in all of the three cases. This is consistent with previous studies which confirm that there is a negative significant correlation between working capital and the level of SR.

The degree of relationship between the age of the MCG and the level of SR is not significant according to Table 4.5. This is clearly visible from the various values of p-values which are all more than 0.05. The correlation between the age of the MCG (LAG) and the level of SR are all weak (r = 0.05 for word, r = 0.16 for pages and r=-0.04 for paragraphs) and insignificant (p-value= 0.81, 0.71, and 0.91 for words, pages and paragraphs respectively). Negative and insignificant relationships were observed between complexity (LCOM) as a corporate characteristic and the level of SR (r=-0.09 with p-value=0.53, r= 0.05 with p-value=0.74, r=-0.08 with p-value=0.59 for words, pages and paragraphs respectively).

Table 4.5 Correlation matrix between the dependent and independent variables

Variables	LWD	LPAG	LPAR	LSZ	LGRO	LPR	LEFF	LGEA	LWOC	LAG	LCOM
LWD	1.00										
LPAG	0.92 (0.00)	1.00									
LPAR	0.60 (0.00)	0.52 (0.00)	1.00								
LSZ	0.69 (0.00)	0.66 (0.00)	0.40 (0.00)	1.00							
LGRO	0.09 (0.52)	0.08 (0.56)	-0.17 (0.23)	0.01 (0.97)	1.00						
LPRO	0.22 (0.13)	0.22 (0.11)	-0.01 (0.95)	0.17 (0.24)	0.18 (0.22)	1.00					

	LWD	LPAG	LPAT	LSZ	LGRO	LPRO	LEFF	LGEA	LWC	LAG	LCOM
LEFF	0.35 (0.01)	0.17 (0.23)	0.18 (0.22)	0.46 (0.00)	0.11 (0.44)	0.03 (0.82)	1.00				
LGEA	0.13 (0.36)	0.05 (0.73)	0.06 (0.70)	0.24 (0.09)	0.09 (0.55)	-0.05 (0.72)	0.02 (0.90)	1.00			
LWC	-0.50 (0.00)	-0.41 (0.00)	-0.30 (0.03)	-0.44 (0.00)	0.15 (0.30)	-0.13 (0.37)	-0.02 (0.87)	-0.41 (0.00)	1.00		
LAG	0.05 (0.73)	0.16 (0.27)	-0.04 (0.80)	0.17 (0.23)	-0.03 (0.83)	0.05 (0.73)	0.20 (0.16)	0.13 (0.37)	0.17 (0.23)	1.00	
LCOM	-0.09 (0.53)	-0.05 (0.74)	-0.08 (0.59)	0.21 (0.15)	-0.05 (0.71)	0.05 (0.73)	0.02 (0.91)	0.16 (0.25)	-0.12 (0.39)	0.36 (0.01)	1.00

Source: Author

Notes:
1. Figures in bracket are the p-values
2. LWD, LPAG and LPAT stand for natural log of words, pages and paragraphs respectively. LSZ, LGRO, LPRO, LEFF, LGEA, LWC, LAG and LCOM denote natural log of size, growth, profitability, efficiency, working capital, age and complexity.

4.8 Regression analysis

Regression analysis is conducted to examine empirically the effects of corporate characteristics on the levels of SR and the management approach disclosures of the GRI. This statistical method is to test the determinants of the level of SR, using the number of words, pages and paragraphs as dependent variables. This was examined by regressing every disclosure variable on each corporate characteristic were scrutinised to determine whether any recognisable pattern (either between types of disclosure and corporate characteristics) could be observed. In each analysis the statistical technique employed was OLS regression (Gray et al., 2001). Ordinary least squares regression (OLS) is a statistical method using sample data to fit the true relationship between a set of independent variables and response (dependent) variable. This method is appropriate when the underlying observations are measured for a particular period. But, when the observations (MCGs) are measured over different times, this method can lead to unreliable estimators. The regression model is described by the formula:

$$Y = f(x) \qquad (1)$$

Where Y is the dependant variable and is a function of x, a vector of independent variables which determine Y. Without verifying that the data have met the assumptions underlying OLS model, the results may be misleading and inappropriate for any valid conclusion. There are a number of assumptions which underlie the OLS model namely normality of residuals, homogeneity of variance (homoscedasticity) and collinearity. These assumptions were examined based on the data from 2008 to 2012 have been discussed in following Sections.

The first general hypothesis, which states that the level of SR (words, pages and paragraph) is some function of one or more of size, growth rate, profitability ratio, efficiency ratio, gearing ratio, working capital ratio, age and complexity of MCGs, was examined by estimating the following equations. The level of disclosure variables (words, pages and paragraphs) were therefore regressed on each of the corporate characteristics for the sample. For example hypothesis that the level of SR in terms of measurement (e.g. Words) is some function of corporate characteristics (e.g. size) over the whole time period from 2008 to 2012 was investigated by regressing each of the seven levels of SR variables on the size characteristics variables. To avoid the problem of heteroscedasticity, ordinary least squares (OLS) regression with heteroscedasticity robust standard errors (Lu, and Abeysekera, 2014) was used to test the relationships implicit in model (1). The results for regression are shown in Table 4.6. The regression model used is shown in equation (1) below:

$$LnSR = \beta_0 + \beta_1 \, lnSize + \beta_2 \, lnGrowth + \beta_3 \, lnProb + \beta_4 \, lnEff$$
$$+ \beta_5 \, ln\,Gear + \beta_6 \, lnWCap + \beta_7 \, lnAge + \beta_8 \, ln\,Complex + \varepsilon$$

Where $LnSR$ represents the level of Sustainability Report and $\beta_1 \, lnSize + \beta_2 \, lnGrowth + \beta_3 \, lnProb + \beta_4 \, lnEff + \beta_5 \, ln\,Gear + \beta_6 \, lnWCap + \beta_7 \, lnAge + \beta_8 \, ln\,Complex$ represent the transformed values of the corporate characteristic of type for MCG. $\beta 0$ is the intercept and the slope coefficient of the regression line, and is the random error term. The random error term is assumed to be independently distributed of each of other error terms and to have zero mean and constant variance. The slope coefficients for the regression of each disclosure variable on the characteristics within the period and the t-values for the two sided test are presented in the various Tables below.

A robust regression model was performed and the results presented in Table 4.6 for (log words, log pages and log paragraphs) of all the eight control variables for the five years from 2008 to 2012. The table indicated that the F-value of each model is statistically significant at the 5% level. This means that the coefficients on all the eight control variables can jointly explain significant variations in the data and they are significantly different from zero. The R-squares for each of the model range from 24% to 63% for all the models for the study period to explain the variations of the determination of the level of SR. These results statistically support the significance of the models for example the R-square of 0.631 is considered to be a good result. This implies that independent variables explain 63.1% of the variances and this correspond favourably with similar studies undertaken for example by Hossain and Hammami, 2009 where the R-square was at 61.7%, Akhtaruddin (2005) at 55.7%, Haniffa and Cooke (2002) at 46.3%, and Ahmed (1996) at 33.2%.

The interpretation of these values is that if this model is applied on a new data set, there would be the same amount of variability accounted for in the data set. It can be seen from the models that all the results shows a varying t-values. The results demonstrate F-values as 35.33 with a Root MSE of 0.47, 23.39 with a Root MSE of 0.43, and 8.15 with a Root MSE of 0.98 for models LWD, LPAG and LPAR respectively which are all statistically significant. This signifies that the predictors (independent variables) did a good job of predicting the outcome variables and can therefore be concluded that there is a significant relationship between the set of predictors and the dependent variables.

Table 4.6 Regression of the characteristics determining the level of SR

Variables	Model 1 Words	Model 2 Pages	Model 3 Paragraphs
LSZ	0.275	0.298	0.274
	(5.70)	(5.36)	(3.35)
LGRO	0.128	0.122	-0.248
	(1.06)	(1.26)	(-0.79)
LPRO	0.034	0.026	-0.065
	(1.56)	(0.98)	(-0.78)
LEFF	0.024	-0.113	0.009
	(0.49)	(-2.31)	(0.09)
LGEA	-0.166	-0.274	-0.218
	(-3.39)	(-4.88)	(-2.98)
LWC	-0.207	-0.149	-0.149
	(-4.91)	(-3.62)	(-2.07)
LAG	0.102	0.201	0.005
	(1.22)	(2.69)	(0.04)
LCOM	-0.470	-0.439	-0.417
	(-2.25)	(-2.30)	(-1.12)
Constant/Intercept	10.090	4.327	9.617
	(18.28)	(8.30)	(9.68)
R-square	0.629	0.608	0.244
F-value	35.33	23.39	8.15
P-value	0.00	0.00	0.00
Root MSE	0.467	0.426	0.977
No. of Observation	50	50	50

Source: Author

Notes:

1. Figures in bracket are the t-values
2. LWD, LPAG and LPAT stand for natural log words, pages and paragraphs respectively. LSZ, LGRO, LPRO, LEFF, LGEA, LWC, LAG and LCOM denote natural log of size, growth, profitability, efficiency, working capital, age and complexity.
3. R-squares were used because adjusted R-square cannot be deduced due the use of robust regression model.

4.8.1 Size of MCG and the level of SR

The size of a company has been of interest to many researchers over the years. It has been classified as one of the characteristics of company and could be regarded as having a relationship with the level of SR. The corporate size has been measured in many ways by previous literature without theoretical justifications for choosing one of them. According to Burgwal and Vieira (2014) the most commonly used measures are number of employees, total assets, sales volume, or an index rank (e.g. Fortune 500). Other studies adopt other two measurement variables to assess corporate size: total revenue (Chau and Gray, 2010, Li et al., 2008; Meek et al., 1995) and market capitalization (Chen and Jaggi, 2000; Leventis and Weetman, 2004). In this study however, the researcher uses revenue as the appropriate indicator for the measurement of size (Gray et al., 2001). The main reason is that most companies are classified according to the amount of revenue that can be made within certain period of time. Corporate size is measured by the natural logarithm of total amount of total revenue owing to positive skewness in the raw measure (Gray et al., 2001). Revenue is measured using the total sales figure for fiscal year (Chau and Gray, 2010, Li et al., 2008; Meek et al., 1995).

Previous studies suggest that large companies disclosed more social and environmental information (Dierkes and Coppock, 1978). The sustainability information is believed to be more in the public eye and is under more scrutiny (Dierkes and Coppock, 1978). Large companies normally adopt Lindblom's (2010) strategies in the process of SR preparation to justify their actions. This is with reference to the findings of the previous studies where there is expected tendency of larger companies to produce more information to justify their actions and behaviours to their stakeholders. Therefore, the first supporting research question is presented as follows: "Are there any effect of MCGs' size on the level of SR?"

Sustainability reporting by larger corporations has been steadily increasing in both size and complexity over the last two decades (Gray et al., 2001). Not only are such disclosures by larger corporations now common place but they are attracting increasing attention from stakeholders and regulators (see for example, Gray et al., 1997; Deegan and Gordon, 1996; Schaltegger, 1996; Elkington, 1997; KPMG, 1997; UNCTAD, 1996; Gray et al., 2001). According to the existing literature, the relationship between size and sustainability disclosures has come out with more consistent results. For example, Gray et al. (2001); Belkaoui and Karpik (1989), Adams et al. (1995 and 1998) and Hackston and Milne (1996) in their respective studies concluded that social and environmental disclosures can be explained by size. On the contrary, however, Singh and Ahuja (1983) find no relationship between size of company and levels of SR. Studies by Cowen et al. (1987) also find that although there are some relationship between size and level of SR it only holds for certain areas of disclosure namely environmental and community-based disclosures.

According to Dainelli et al. (2013), the general agreement regarding the existence of a positive relationship between the size of a company and the level of its disclosure, is explain by several reasons. First, company size affects voluntary financial disclosure by influencing the magnitude of agency costs (Holthausen and Leftwich, 1983, Dainelli et al., 2013; Kelly, 1983 and Leftwich et al., 1981). Second, larger companies are considered to be able to afford both direct and indirect disclosure costs compared to smaller companies (Meek et al., 1995). Finally, financial analysts observed that larger companies are more visible to the community than others and this put pressure on the company to release more information (Schipper, 1991; Dainelli et al., 2013). Consequently, many studies highlight a positive relationship between firm size and the level of disclosure (Dainelli et al., 2013; Abdullah and Ku Ismail, 2008 and Watson et al., 2002). Therefore the study hypothesizes that MCGs size is positively related to the level of SR.

The Table 4.6 shows the results from the regression model of the number of words, pages and paragraphs on the independent variables. The empirical evidence derived from the regression model indicates that size is statistically related to the level of SR in terms of number of words, pages and paragraphs with significant (t-value>1.68) positive coefficient. It can be seen from the results that the R-square of 0.629 is very good value and 63% of variation in the dependent variable are explained by the independent variables. The model also shows that there is significant influence of size on both the number of words pages and paragraphs (t-values =5.70, 5.36, and 3.35, respectively). There is a positive relationship with a coefficient of 0.275 for words, 0.298 for pages and 0.274 for paragraphs. The result also shows the level of SR is positively affected by corporate size with respect to all the three measurements. In this case the bigger the size of an MCG the higher the level of information disclosed on the SR. This is inconsistence with study by Dainelli et al. (2013) using size measured as total revenue which does not show any significant relationship results but consistent when market capitalization is used as a measure. This means that the level of internationalization and external visibility on company disclosure strategies have influence on the results (Cahan et al., 2005; Dainelli et al. (2013).

4.8.2 Growth rates and the level of SR

Another factor, which is closely linked with size, is growth rate measured in terms of the extent of a firm's asset and investment in R&D (Artiach et al., 2010). Product and process innovation resulting from R&D can lead to corporate sustainability related processes and products, resulting in improved processes that will make them more effective (Padgett and Galan 2010; Lourenço and Branco, 2013). According to Padgett and Galan (2010), the improved processes are likely to reduce the amount of energy consumed by the company and this will lead to cost reductions and less pollution (Padgett and Galan, 2010) therefore facilitate the growth of the company. Artiach et al. (2010) argue that it is more likely that a company with a higher level of growth options in its asset mix to be able to incorporate sustainability principles into its competitive strategy that will affect the level of SR.

As far as the previous literature is concerned, only few studies were found to have assessed the relationship between growth rate and the level of SR. There are many factors that can affect a company that is on the verge of growth namely, the loyalty of new customers, the acceptance of the communities around, the commitments and satisfaction of the employees, the trust of new suppliers and creditors. MCG with the larger growing rate is expected to demonstrate a sustained socially desirable picture to their stakeholders, hence the preparation of SR to achieve that. Research and development will bring about product and process innovation which can lead to improved processes and more effective of doing things (Padgett and Galan 2010; Lourenço and Branco, 2013). This means that firm's growth rate and corporate sustainability performance are positively related (Lourenço and Branco, 2013). This brings up the second research question which is concerned with whether growing MCGs disclose more information on SR than non-growing MCGs. The question specifically asks: "Are there any effect of MCGs' growth rates and the level of SR?"

According to Table 4.6 the growth rate is not significant in influencing all the dependent variables with all the t-values less than 1.68 with varying coefficients (0.128, 0.122 and -0.248 for words, pages and paragraphs respectively). It is obvious that the type of relationship between the growth rate and dependent variables as given in Table 4.6 is linear.

4.8.3 Profitability ratio and the level of SR

The next feature that the study wants to investigate is profitability ratio and the level of SR which has been used by many researchers over the years (Kemp, 2001: Utaminingtyas and Ahalik, 2010). There are few researches that have studied the relationship between CSR and the company profitability especially in the developing countries (Kemp, 2001). Several profitability measures have been used in disclosure literature to measure a firm's profitability (Dainelli et al., 2013). With respect to profitability, according to Burgwal and Vieira (2014) many previous studies have adopted single year accounting measures (Freedman and Jaggi, 1982) and multiple year averages in the measurement (Cowen et al., 1987; Hackston and Milne, 1996). A more reliable measure of profitability is the use of an extended period (Hackston and Milne, 1996). In this study the five-year average return on equity (EBIT/total equity) is used as a measure for profitability (Burgwal and Vieira, 2014). This is because most used capital return measures; the "net profit on equity" is the most widespread index (Cahan et al., 2005; Chau and Gray, 2010; Chavent et al., 2006; Eng and Mak, 2003; Haniffa and Cooke, 2002; Ho and Wong, 2001; Lim et al., 2007, Owusu-Ansah, 1998; Patton and Zelenka, 1997; Raffournier, 1995), followed by the "net profit on total assets" (Cahan et al., 2005; Eng and Mak, 2003; McNally et al., 1982 and Wang et al., 2008).

Some of the findings from these studies suggest that the level of disclosure in SR have certain relationship with the performance of the companies (McGuire et al., 1986). Many studies agreed that looking for the relationship between SR and firm profitability will have some policy implications. In the first instance, if the company's financial performance has a positive effect on the level of SR, the company should consider more on the existing CSR practices. On the other hand if there is a negative effect of the company's financial performance on the level of SR, then the company should assess the ineffectiveness CSR practices and adopt a corrective measure to deal with them.

According to Gray et al. (2001) the relationship between profitability ratio and these sustainability disclosures, if it exists, proves to be elusive. Studies conducted by Hackston and Milne (1996) and Belkaoui and Karpik (1989) found no relationship between profit and the level of SR. However, Freedman and Ullmann (1986) and Freedman and Jaggi (1988) find either no relationship or an inverse relationship. On the other hand, Anderson and Frankle (1980) and Bowman (1978) finds a positive relationship between social disclosure and financial performance with Abbott and Monsen (1979) find no effects of profitability on the level of sustainability report.

Many previous researches agreed that most profitable companies are more likely to have higher level of social and environmental information and therefore have positively relationship with profitability of the company (Roberts, 1992; Gray et al., 1999). In the views of Utaminingtyas and Ahalik (2010) there is a significant effect of CSR on the Earning Response Coefficient (ERC). ERC is the response of stock return to differentiation between expectation and actual earnings (Walter et al. 1996; Kothari and Collins, 1989; Utaminingtyas and Ahalik, 2010). The term is used in a generic sense to measure the degree of co-movement between security returns and shocks to an earnings series without necessarily implying that the latter cause the former (Kothari and Collins, 1989). It is evidently clear from the above that there is an increasing level of sustainability reporting among companies. Even though, this increase is suggestive of companies' intentions to be more open and transparent to their stakeholders. It is expected that companies have to take actions to ensure that adequacy and transparency of the sustainability information are available to the general public in the form of reports. In the view of Davis (1973) and Soloman and Hansen (1985) they also agreed that CSR will be goodwill for a company in the long run. In contrast, Johnsen and Gjoelberg (2009) in their research found that CSR could have a negative effect on the firm financial performance. In this regard it can be argued that the relationship between CSR and company's performance is still inconclusive (Griffin and Mahon, 1997; Margolis et al., 2007). Therefore, the third research question is: "Are there any effect profitability of the MCG on the level of SR?"

From Table 4.6 it can be seen that the effect of the profitability ratio on the level of SR is not significant with all the models. It can be seen from the table that all the t-values are less than 1.68 (t-values 1.56 for words, 0.98 for pages and -0.78 for paragraphs). These indicate that there is no effect of profitability ratio on level of SR with respect to all the models meaning MCGs with profitability are likely to affect SR. This result is inconsistent with studies where companies with higher profitability ratio provide more explanations regarding their results than other firms (Aerts and Cheng, 2012; Brennan et al., 2009; Clatworthy and Jones, 2003; Dainelli et al., 2013).

This means that the result is consistent with several studies according to Dainelli et al. (2013) where signalling strategies and empirical evidence shows conflicting results. For example, some studies highlight a positive relationship between a company's profitability and its level of disclosure (Gamerschlag et al., 2011, Haniffa and Cooke, 2002, Lim et al., 2007 and Wang et al., 2008), while other literature finds no relationship (Alsaeed, 2006, Cahan et al., 2005, Chau and Gray, 2002, Chau and Gray, 2010, Eng and Mak, 2003, Ho and Wong, 2001, Hossain and Hammami, 2009, Malone et al., 1993, McNally et al., 1982, Meek et al., 1995, Patelli and Prencipe, 2007; Raffournier, 1995; Dainelli et al., 2013) which is the case of this study. The main reason for these inconclusive results may be because these studies aim to investigate how corporate characteristics influence the amount of disclosure included in annual reports and they develop disclosure indexes that encompass different topics (see Botosan, 1997, Meek et al., 1995; Wallace and Naser, 1995; Dainelli et al., 2013). Another reason may be that all the companies under investigation are subsidiaries who take instructions from head office to prepare or not to prepare SR.

4.8.4 Efficiency ratio and the level of SR

There are few previous studies that have investigated the association between managerial efficiency (i.e. asset turnover) and the level of SR (Waddock et al., 1997; Bouten et al., 2012; Parsa and Kouhy, 2001; Lu and Abeysekera 2014). Studies by Sturdivant and Ginter (1977), Orlitzky et al. (2003) and Bird et al. (2007) found that CSR practices adopted by companies could have a positive effect on their efficiency of activities. This is because companies with a higher level of disclosure have been attributed to have a better image and therefore, are regarded by stakeholders such as investors, lenders and banks as a lower risk company. Therefore, the third research question is: "Are there any effect of managerial efficiency on the level of SR?" The effect of efficiency ratio on the levels of SR was seen to be statistically not significant in all the SR measurements as given in Table 4.6 apart from number of pages. This means that efficiency of management of MCGs seems not to have any effect on the information disclosed in the sustainability report with respect to both number of words and paragraphs.

4.8.5 Capital gearing ratio and the level of SR

Capital gearing ratio measures the ratio of total debt to equity of a company (Gray et al., 2001). It is used to measure the level of risk level of a company and have been divided into two components: 1) operational risk, measured by the weight of intangible assets and 2) financial risk, measured by leverage ratio (Dainelli et al., 2013; Patton and Zelenka, 1997). In this study, gearing is measured by the leverage ratio which is the total debt to equity (Gray et al., 2001). The empirical evidence in disclosure literature shows a conflicting result regarding the relationship between the gearing ratio and levels of SR. Research conducted by Garsombke (1979) and Firth (1984) did not find any correlation between the risk level, measured by the beta index, and the amount of voluntary communication in the annual report. Beta is a measure of the volatility, or systematic risk, of a security or a portfolio in comparison to the market as a whole (Garsombke, 1979; Firth, 1984). It is used in the capital asset pricing model (CAPM), a model that calculates the expected return of an asset based on its beta and expected market returns (Garsombke, 1979; Firth, 1984).

Furthermore, in a related study by Patton and Zelenka (1997) who investigated the determinants of disclosure in annual reports had their results indicating that neither of the two risk proxies they used as measurement of risk is significantly related to disclosure practices. However, in the view of Aupperle et al. (1985) many existing studies suggest that companies with a lower risk (i.e. lower gearing) disclose more social information than those with high risk. This means that lower gearing companies disclose more social and environmental information to justify their actions by adopting any of Lindblom's (2010) four strategies. On the contrary, according to agency theory, a positive relationship between the risk level and the extent of disclosure may be expected: owing to higher proprietary costs, higher risk firms are likely to disclose more information than others (Dainelli et al., 2013).

In viewing the foregoing discussion in Hahn and Kühnen (2013), they stated that the existing empirical results are rather mixed. A high level of indebtedness, leverage, or gearing can be assumed to decrease the ability and flexibility of a company to bear the costs of reporting and/or face the consequences of disclosing potentially damaging information (e.g., Cormier and Magnan, 2003; Stanny and Ely, 2008). In the view of Haniffa and Cooke (2005) however, they also argue that sustainability reporting might be used to legitimize corporate activities toward creditors and shareholders, thus providing incentives to engage in reporting. In line with this study a positive relationship between gearing ratio (risk level) and the level of disclosure on SR is hypothesized because sustainability disclosure is considered highly relevant information (Dainelli et al., 2013). As noted from the Table 4.6 the statistical analysis provide a significant impact of the capital gearing ratio on sustainability information (t-value=-3.39 for words, t-value=-4.88 for pages and t-value=-2.98 for paragraphs). The effect of gearing on the SR is negative as far as all the measurements of SR are concerned (-0.166 for number of words, -0.274 for pages and -0.218 for paragraphs). These show that the number of words, pages and paragraphs in SR move in opposite direction with the gearing ratio with significant effect. This means that the level of SR is likely to be lower as the gearing ratio becomes larger.

The negative coefficient of capital gearing is inconsistent with theoretical and empirical expectations. Specifically, it was reported by Bevan and Danbolt, (2002; 2004) that there is a statistically significant positive relationship between gearing and the level of SR. The study is also inconsistent with study by Dainelli et al., (2013) where it was found there is a positive sign for the risk coefficient, thereby meaning that higher risk (highly geared) companies are more inclined to publish performance indicators although variable is not a significant determinant for level of disclosure. However, in the view of Hahn and Kühnen (2013) existing empirical results are rather mixed. A high level of indebtedness, leverage, or gearing can be assumed to decrease the ability and flexibility of a company to bear the costs of reporting and/or face the consequences of disclosing potentially damaging information (e.g., Cormier and Magnan, 2003; Stanny and Ely, 2008). This seem consistent with the result of this study. In the view of Haniffa and Cooke (2005) however, they also argue that sustainability reporting might be used to legitimize corporate activities toward creditors and shareholders, thus providing incentives to engage in reporting.

4.8.6 Working capital and the level of SR

The term working capital is a financial yardstick which represents operating liquidity available to a business (Modi 2012). It is calculated as current assets minus current liabilities. If current assets are less than current liabilities, an entity has a working capital deficiency, also called a working capital deficit (Modi 2012). According to Wallace and Naser (1995) regulatory institutions as well as investors and lenders are concerned with the going concern status of companies. Hence a firm's ability to honour its short-term obligations as they fall due, without recourse to selling other assets in-place, is expected. In studies by Belkaoui-Riahi and Kahl (1978), and also Cooke (1989), it was indicated that highly liquid companies are associated with greater levels of disclosure, although Wallace et al. (1994) argued that companies with a low liquidity position might disclose more information to justify their liquidity status.

Furthermore, whereas Belkaoui-Riahi (1978) found no relationship between working capital ratio (liquidity) and the level of disclosure, Wallace et al. (1994) had a significant negative association between working capital ratio and levels of disclosure for listed and unlisted Spanish companies. These findings suggest empirical literature as inconclusive. On the part of Wallace and Naser (1995), Owusu-Ansah (1998) and Oyelere et al. (2003) they also suggested that company liquidity is an important determinant of corporate disclosure. Thus in the light of legitimacy theory, there exists a negative relationship between environmental disclosure and liquidity of a firm. On the other hand, Ho and Taylor (2007) state that according to signalling theory, highly liquid companies may have stronger incentives to provide more details in their corporate disclosures about their abilities to meet short-term financial obligations. Thus, it predicts a positive association between disclosure and firm's liquidity position.

It can be seen from the Table 4.6 that all the coefficients are having a negative value which suggest that the level of SR move in the opposite direction with the working capital ratio of the MCG. According to the table the effect of working capital on SR are highly significant (t-value>1.68) with all the models. This means it is expected to observe a lower level of SR when the working capital ratio goes up. This is consistent with Wallace et al. (1994) where they found that working capital (liquidity) has significant and negative coefficient, suggesting that companies with lower liquidity disclose more information to justify their liquidity position (Wallace et al.,

1994). This result is consistent with the legitimacy theory of environmental disclosure.

In a study by Belkaoui-Riahi and Kahl (1978) and Cooke (1989) it was indicated that highly liquid companies is associated with greater levels of disclosure although in the view of Wallace et al. (1994) it was argued that companies with a low liquidity position might disclose more information to justify their liquidity status. Furthermore, whereas Belkaoui- Riahi (1978) found no relationship between working capital ratio (liquidity) and the level of disclosure, Wallace et al. (1994) had a significant negative association between working capital ratio and levels of disclosure for listed and unlisted Spanish companies. These findings suggest empirical literature as inconclusive and support the findings of this study that there is inconsistency in the literature. In a related development according to Hahn and Kühnen (2013) sustainability reporting may be positively influenced by financing activities on the capital market. This means companies trying to raise capital may use SR as a means to reduce information asymmetry between a company and its investors, thereby also lowering costs of capital (Hahn and Kühnen, 2013). Cormier and Magnan (2003) and Clarkson et al. (2008) find a positive effect on the extent or quality specifically of sustainability reporting, but on the contrary, Clarkson et al. (2011) and Cormier and Magnan (2004) indicate no significant influence.

4.8.7 Age of the MCG and the level of SR

The age of the MCG is defined as the number of years the company has been in operation (Hossain and Hammami, 2009). The extent of SR may be influenced by the age of the MCG (stage of development and growth) and in principle can be offered as an independent variable in explaining the level of SR (Owusu-Ansah, 1998). Many previous studies including Akhtaruddin (2005), Haniffa and Cooke (2002), Glaum and Street (2003) and Hossain (2008) found that there is an insignificance relationship in explaining the level of disclosure and the age of a company. In the view of Owusu-Ansah (1998) longer-established firm will tend to disclose more information than more newly-established firm. The possible reasons for that can be explained with the studies by Owusu-Ansah (1998) where three points were argued. In that study the author argued that younger companies may suffer competitive disadvantage if they disclose certain items such as information on research expenditure, capital expenditure, and product development. Secondly, these costs are likely to be more onerous for younger companies than for their older counterparts. Finally, there is a situation that younger companies may lack a 'track record' to rely on for public disclosure and therefore may have less information to disclose or less rich disclosures.

The statistical analysis from the models results from Table 4.6 shows that the age of the MCG have insignificant impact (t-value<1.68) on the level of SR with respect to all but number of pages measurements. The previous research studies of Akhtaruddin (2005), Haniffa and Cooke (2002), Glaum and Street (2003) and Hossain (2008) found age of a company as insignificance in explaining the level of disclosure which is consistent with this study to some extent. The possible reasons for results can be explained with the studies by Owusu-Ansah (1998) where three points were argued. In the studies the author argued that younger companies may suffer competitive disadvantage if they disclose certain items such as information on research expenditure, capital expenditure, and product development. Secondly, these costs are likely to be more onerous for younger companies than for their older counterparts. Finally, there is a situation that younger companies may lack a 'track record' to rely on for public disclosure and therefore may have less information to disclose or less rich disclosures. These assertions seem to explain some of the reasons of the results (Owusu-Ansah, 1998).

4.8.8 Complexity of the MCG and the level of SR

Complexity as one of the corporate characteristics is used to measure the extent to which companies have subsidiaries (Hossain and Hammami, 2009). The degree of complexity variable is measured by the number of subsidiaries a company has both in host and foreign countries can be used to examine the impact of on the level of SR. In a study by Zarzeski (1996) it was argued that companies which have international presence may provide higher levels of disclosure in practices than their domestic counterparts. The study of Haniffa and Cooke (2002) suggested that structural complexity may be significant in explaining variability in the extent of disclosure. In the same view, according to Depoers (2000), operating in a number of geographical areas including other countries increases the amount of information controlled by such company and therefore will increase the level of SR. Riahi-Belkaoui (2001) also agree that there are positive association between disclosure and the extent of complexity of the companies. Based on the above arguments, the author hypothesize the level of SR is positively associated with the complexity of the firm.

Table 4.6 shows that complexity as a corporate characteristic is significant (t-value >1.68) for all apart from number of paragraphs as a measurements. It is obvious that the type of relationship between the complexity of the MCGs and the level of SR in terms of number of words, and pages is important in influencing the level of SR. The coefficients of complexity are negative and statistically significant. This implies that MCGs which has a lot of subsidiaries do not seem to produce high level of SR. According to the results the more complex an MCG is the lesser information that may be disclosed on SR than a company with no such subsidiaries. This is inconsistent with studies like Hossain and Mitra (2004), Hossain (2001) and Hossain and Reaz (2007) which found positive influence on the environmental disclosure. Although the results concerning the degree of complexity revealed that there is negative associated with the level of SR, it is considered to be inconsistent with the previous findings of Branco and Rodrigues (2008). This indicated the absence of a relationship between how many subsidiaries a company may have and level of SR. Further, it is also not consistent with the findings of Stanny and Ely (2008). The negative effect of complexity of the MCGs on the level of SR, may be due to the probability that the having many subsidiaries in developing countries does not mean more attention are be paid to the social responsibility by these companies.

4.9 Conclusion

The researcher has a view that there are a number of factors beyond the technicalities of research design and methods. Therefore it is important to make it clear here the researcher's philosophical assumption before the discussion of research methods to be employed. Research methods are the process in which data is collected. Even though there are two main methods namely, quantitative and qualitative research which is known to be alternative strategies, they are not mutually exclusive since the two of them can be used at the same time within one research but the study adopted a quantitative research approach where content analysis was used.

Social and environmental disclosure may also take place through different media (Bouten et al., 2012). Even though most research into such disclosure tends to use data contained within the corporation's annual report, there are wide range of other media that may be employed: advertising, focus groups, employee councils, booklets, schools education and so forth (see, for example, Zeghal and Ahmed, 1990). The total population of this research is the annual reports of all the MCGs (e.g., stand alone or combined reports). Many previous studies have used the annual reports in analysing the adequacy of SR in the past (e.g., Campbell, 2000, 2004; Beck et al., 2010; Bouten et al., 2011). There are two main reasons for using the annual reports for the analysis according to Bouten et al., (2011). In the first place, in discharging their accountability functions companies usually use annual reports to communicate with their stakeholders (Gray et al., 1995; Adams et al., 1998; Neu et al,. 1998) and it is believed to be widely distributed and often directly available on website. This study, in keeping with prior research is restricted to annual report disclosures (Gray et al., 2001).

The relevant empirical literature on the first main research question was reviewed in earlier. Each of these eight sections presented a review of the relevant literature on one corporate characteristic and focused on whether there was any evidence of the effect on the level of sustainability information disclosure in the SR. Chapter was then continued by reviewing the relevant literature on eight corporate characteristics (i. e. size, profitability, growth rate, efficiency, gearing, working capital, age and complexity of the MCGs) and the level of sustainability report. The literature review revealed that most of the previous studies have focused on the social and environmental activities of companies.

Chapter 5

Managerial and Policy Implications

5.1 Introduction

In this concluding chapter, the aims and objectives of the study are reiterated. It also presented a brief a summary of the main findings together with concluding remarks is presented. It also provides a section on the scope of the study and outlines the limitations that were experienced over the course of conducting this research and recommendations for further research and further comments are presented.

5.2 The main findings and conclusion

The overall finding of this study suggests that in the absence of any requirements by the regulatory bodies, MCGs' sustainability reporting is depended on their corporate characteristics. This means that there are some of effects of corporate characteristics on the level of disclosure in sustainability report absence of any regulatory requirements in Ghana and that MCGs use SR disclosure for legitimacy purposes. Based on the empirical findings, it was argued that MCGs could have adopted any of Lindblom's four strategies when preparing SR. The overall finding for the research question can be interpreted as MCGs disclosing SR to legitimise their corporate behaviours to their stakeholders. More detailed of these findings are as follows:

a) The empirical evidence was found to suggest that the size of the MCG have some effect on the level of SR in all the measurement. This finding suggests that larger MCGs disclosed more information in their SR than smaller companies. This finding was also consistent with the findings of the earlier studies where it was argued that larger companies are more in the public eye, and therefore are more likely to disclose more information on their sustainability report. According to the study larger companies disclose more information, either to justify their behaviours to their stakeholders or to indicate that they have the same norms and values as those of the society. In this vain it can be concluded that companies could have adopted the first, second or the fourth strategy introduced by Lindblom (2010).
b) No association was observed between corporate growth rate and the level of sustainability report within the period under consideration. According to the results corporate growth rate do not determine the level of information disclosure in the SR.
c) There is also no effect of profitability on the amount of information in the SR within the five years according to the results. This observation which was not in alignment with the overall perception given by the previous studies was explained by the fact that this study did not measure the extent of formation disclosed by these mining companies.
d) The evidence also showed that, the efficiency of the MCGs does not have significant effect on the level of disclosure in the SR (see Table 4.6). This means that the MCGs with better managerial systems in place have no influence on the level of disclosure in the SR. When no regulatory code of best practice had been introduced on how companies should disclose sustainability information there was still no association of efficiency of management on the level of SR. The evidence also suggests that mining companies were not using sustainability information to assure their investors that managers were acting in their best interests. Instead, the no impact of efficiency of management on sustainability information being disclosed in the SR clearly suggested that in the absence of any regulations, MCGs are not disclosing more sustainability information as may have been predicted.
e) There is a significant negative effect of capital gearing ratio on the level of SR according to the results. This reflects that highly geared

MCGs are more likely to provide lesser level of SR. Ownership-diffusion means that there is a diversity of shareholders' needs for information about the social responsibility of companies.
f) The results appear to explain the existence of negative relationship between working capital ratio and the level of SR by the mining companies. The statistically significant coefficients on working capital indicate that they do have significant impact on the level of SR. The results imply that companies with more working capital do not necessarily disclose higher level of SR but rather less information on SR. Overall, it offers further empirical support to the results of the descriptive analyses that companies' working capital, impact negatively on the levels of SR.
g) The ages of the MCGs was also found to have no effect on the level of SR. One of the possible reasons for the results is that most of the MCGs were formed through merger or acquisition of existing companies whiles other were form from the scratch to the extent that reporting a voluntary report may be a matter of policy. Therefore the age a company may not be a determining factor for reporting.
h) The findings of the research also suggest that there is effect of complexity of the MCGs on the level of SR. The evidence revealed that the number of subsidiary a MCGs may have, both at home and/or abroad, is likely to affect the level of SR. The effect of complexity of the MCGs on the level of SR means that MCGs with many subsidiaries rather disclose less level of sustainability reports. This is consistent with a suggested framework, may be due to the probability that having many subsidiaries in developing countries do not mean more attention will be paid to the social responsibility by the MCG.

5.3 Managerial and policy implications

The results from this study can be said to have many managerial and policy implications for future practitioners in the field of sustainability reporting in particular and CSR in general in Ghana.

a) The results presented in Chapter 4 suggest that there is significant evidence that the level of SR depends on the corporate characteristic of the MCGs to some extent. However, the absence of regulatory framework has contributed to the failure of MCGs to achieve its core aims in term of sustainability reporting. This has contributed to the lack of adequate accountability to stakeholders and to promote change in organisations' social and environmental performance. This raises the fundamental question of whether real change to the sustainability reporting practices could be accomplished through the current climate of voluntarism. The findings suggest several courses of action to ensure an efficient monitoring of the balance of social, environmental and economic performance of organisations to consequently achieve accountability to their stakeholders.

b) There is a need for political head to intervene to regulate (see Zadek et al., 2004) sustainability reporting processes in Ghana. The role would be focus mainly on their duty to counteract the interest of influential stakeholders to ensure that the government acts in society's interest by promoting stakeholder-centred sustainability reporting practices rather than protecting the interests of only organisations. In other words, it will be necessary to develop a better understanding of the appropriate structures of accountability needed to hold corporate power to account with the introduction of legislations and statutory authorities (see also Mulgan, 2000, p563).

c) Another important practical implication is the need for a clear form of social organisation around issues of corporate power and the social and environmental impacts that corporations create as a results of their activities. There should be a fundamental role for civil society groups working in partnership with these mining companies. Through the influence of these groups, the voluntary practice of sustainability reporting could develop towards a stakeholder-centred approach. Their work will also be critical if the practice is to be standardized to ensure that different reporting needs are addressed. However, to counter corporate power it is essential that individuals within these groups become better informed on the role of sustainability reporting practices. In other words, we need a form of structured social regulation (see Zadek, 2007), a network whereby civil society groups could coordinate effective actions to influence social, economic and environmental performance of the companies in the mining sector.

5.4 Conclusion

The research made some contributions to the body of academic knowledge in sustainability reporting practices. The fact that the study investigates the possibility of effect of corporate characteristics on the level of SR assisted in broadening the understandings of why SR is prepared by MCGs in the absence of any legal or regulatory requirements.

The overall finding of this study suggests that in the absence of any requirements by the regulatory bodies, MCGs prepare their sustainability reports according to the type of characteristics associated with it. This suggests that there are some of effects of corporate characteristics on the level of sustainability report in the absence of any regulatory requirements in Ghana and that MCGs use SR disclosure for legitimacy purposes. The empirical findings, gave credence to the fact that MCGs could have adopted any of Lindblom's four strategies when preparing SR. The overall finding for the first main research question can be interpreted as MCGs disclosing SR to legitimise their corporate behaviours to their stakeholders.

This study contributed to the existing knowledge by providing evidence that MCGs must recognise the informational needs of their stakeholders in the preparation of SR. The findings of the study also provided evidence on the changing level of SR prepared by MCGs over the last five year period. It unveiled in particular which of the sustainability information is increasingly been disclosed in relation to the management approach disclosure. The evidence shed light on the question whether there were any indications of MCGs becoming more transparent as suggested in the sustainability argument of Elkington (1999). This will help policy makers in their direction as to what areas of the reports needs to be sensitized to improve its disclosure as it revealed the extent of the economic, social and environmental performance indicators in the reports. Thereby showing areas that need to be encouraged to broaden their reporting to provide more information on a wider range of factors and the direct and indirect economic contributions to the local economies in which they operate.

Concentration on the economy of Ghana, which as a developing country, may constitute a balancing effort and may make it possible to transfer some of the resulting insights to other developing countries (or at least to their researchers). The fact that the study is limited to mining companies in Ghana does not mean, however, that the recommendations cannot be applied to other companies such as manufacturing, banks, investment and insurance although care must be taken in such generalisations.

REFERENCES

Abbott W. F. and Monsen, I. J. (1979). On the measurement of corporate social responsibility: self-reported disclosures as a method of measuring corporate social involvement. **Academy of Management Journal**, 22 (3) pp. 501-515.

Abdullah, A., Ku Ismail, K.N.I. (2008). Disclosure of voluntary accounting ratios by Malaysian listed companies. **Journal of Financial Reporting & Accounting**, 6, (1), pp. 1-20

Adams C. A., Coutts, A. and Harte, G. (1995). Corporate equal opportunities (non-) disclosure. **British Accounting Review**, 27(2) pp 87-108.

Adams C. A., Hill, W. Y. and Roberts, C. B (1998). Corporate social reporting practices in western European: legitimate corporate behaviour? **British, Accounting Review**, 30 (1) March, pp 1-21.

Adams C. A., Hill, W. Y. and Roberts, C. B. (1995). **Environmental, Employee and Ethical Reporting in Europe**. London: (ACCA).

Adams, C and Harte, G (2000). "Making Discrimination Visible: The Potential for Social Accounting", Accounting Forum, Elsevier Science Publishing Company, Inc.

Adams, C. A. (2004). The ethical, social and environmental reporting performance portrayal gap. **Accounting, Auditing and Accountability Journal**, 17 (5) pp. 731-757.

Adams, C. A., & McNicholas, P. (2007). Making a difference: Sustainability reporting, accountability and organisational change. Accounting, Auditing & Accountability Journal, 20(3), pp. 382-402.

Adams, C. A., and Whelan, G. (2009). Conceptualising future change in corporate sustainability reporting. **Accounting, Auditing & Accountability Journal**, 22(1), pp. 118-143.

Adams, C.A. (2002) Internal Organisational Factors Influencing Corporate Social and Ethical Reporting: Beyond Current Theorising. **Accounting, Auditing and Accountability Journal**, 15 (2) pp. 223–250.

Adams, C.A. and Frost, G.R. (2008). Integrating sustainability reporting into management practices. **Accounting Forum**, 32 pp. 288-302.

Adler, R. W. and Milne, M.J (1997). Media exposure, company size, industry, and social disclosure practices. 5th International Perspectives on Accounting (IPA)

Aerts, W & Cheng, P (2012). Self-serving causal disclosures and short-term IPO valuation – evidence from China, Accounting and Business Research, 42, pp.49-75.

Aerts, W., and Cormier, D. (2009). Media legitimacy and corporate environmental communication. **Accounting, Organizations and Society**, 34 (1) pp. 1-27.

Aerts, W., Cormier, D. and Magnan, M. (2008). Corporate Environmental Disclosure, Financial Markets and the Media: An International Perspective. **Ecological Economics**, 64 (3), pp. 643–59.

Akhtaruddin, M (2005). Corporate mandatory disclosure practices in Bangladesh The International Journal of Accounting, 40, pp. 399-422.

Ali, S. H. (2006). Gold mining and tethe golden rule: a challenge for producers and consumers in developing countries. **Journal of Cleaner Production,** 14 (3–4), pp. 455–462.

Alsaeed, K. (2006). The association between firm-specific characteristics and disclosure: The case of Saudi Arabia. **Managerial Auditing Journal**, 21 (5) pp. 476–496.

Al-Shammari, B (2008). Voluntary disclosure in Kuwait corporate annual reports, **Review of Business Research**. 1 (1), 10-30

Al-Tuwaijri, S. A., Christensen, T. E., and Hughes, K. E. II (2004). The relations among environmental disclosure, environmental performance, and economic performance: a simultaneous equations approach. **Accounting, Organizations and Society**, 29 (5/6), pp. 447-471.

Anderson, J. C., and Frankel, A. W. (1980). Voluntary social reporting: An ISO-beta portfolio analysis. **The Accounting Review**, 15(3), pp.467–479.

Archel, P., Fernández, M. and Larrinaga, C. (2008). The organizational and operational boundaries of triple bottom line reporting: A survey. **Environmental Management,** 41 (1), pp. 106–117.

Artiach, T., Lee, D., Nelson, D. and Walker, J. (2010). The determinants of corporate sustainability performance. **Accounting and Finance**, 50 pp. 31-51.

Aupperle K. E., Carroll, A. B. and Hatfield, J. D. (1985). An Empirical Examination of The Relationship Between Corporate Social Responsibility and Profitability. **Academy of management Journal**, 28 (2) pp 446-463.

Azapagic, A. (2004). Developing a framework for sustainable development indicators for the mining and minerals industry. **Journal of Cleaner Production** 12 (6) pp. 639-662.

Baker H. K and Haslem J.A (1974). The impact of investor socioeconomic characteristics on risk and return preferences. **Journal of Business Research**, 2, pp. 469-476.

Ball, A. and Grubnic, S. (2007) Sustainability accounting and accountability in the public sector. In: Unerman, J., Bebbington, J., O'Dwyer, B. (Eds.), **Sustainability Accounting and Accountability.** Routledge, New York, NY, pp. 243-265.

Barako, D. G., Hancock, P. and Izan, H. Y. (2006). Factors Influencing Voluntary Corporate Disclosure by Kenyan Companies. **Corporate Governance**, 14 (2) March, pp. 107-125.

Barret M. E. (1976). Disclosure and Comprehensiveness in an International Setting. **Journal of Accounting Review**, 14, pp. 10-26

Bartels, W., Iansen-Rogers, J. and Kuszewski, J. (2008). Count me in: the readers' take on sustainability reporting, KPMG and SustainAbility. Available from: http://www.globalreporting.org/NR/rdonlyres/3F57ACC-60D0-48F0-AF28-527F85A2A4B4/0/CountMeIn.pdf (Accessed July 5, 2012).

Bartiaux, F. (2008). Does environmental information overcome practice compartmentalisation and change consumers' behaviours? **Journal of Cleaner Production**, 16 (11) pp. 1170-1180.

Beattie, V., and Thomson, S. J. (2007, June). Lifting the lid on the use of content analysis to investigate intellectual capital disclosures. **In Accounting Forum** 31, (2), pp. 129-163.

Bebbington, J., Larrinaga, C. and Moneva, J. M. (2008). Corporate Social Reporting and Reputation Risk Management. **Accounting, Auditing and Accountability Journal**, 21 (3) pp. 337–361.

Beck, A. C., Campbell, D., and Shrives, P. J. (2010). Content analysis in environmental reporting research: enrichment and rehearsal of the method in a British-German context. **The British Accounting Review**, 42 (3) pp. 207-222.

Belkaoui A. and Karpik, P. G. (1989). Determinants of the Corporate Decision to Disclose social Information. **Accounting, Auditing and. Accountability Journal**, 2 (1) pp. 36-51.

Belkaoui, R (1984) Socio- Economic accounting, Praeger Pub. Text

Bellringer, A., Ball, A. and Craig, R. (2011). Reasons for sustainability reporting by New Zealand local governments. **Sustainability Accounting, Management and Policy Journal** 2 pp. 126-138.

Beloe, S., Elkington, J., Hester, K.F., Loose, M. and Zollinger, P. (2006). Tomorrow's Value: The Global Reporters 2006 Survey of Corporate Sustainability Reporting. SustainAbility, London.

Benjamin, J. J. and Stanga, K. G. (1977). Difference in Disclosure Needs of Major Users of Financial Statements. **Accounting and Business Research**, Summer, pp. 187-192.

Berle, A. and G. Means, (1932). The Modern Corporation and Private Property (New York, Macmillan).

Bevan, A.A. & Danbolt, J (2004). Testing for inconsistencies in the estimation of UK capital structure determinants. Applied Financial Economics, 14(1), pp. 55-66.

Bird, R., Hall, A.D., Momentè, F, &Reggiani, F. (2007). What Corporate Social Responsibility Activities are Valued by the Market?, **J Bus Ethics,** 76, pp. 189-206.

Bondy, K., Matten, D. and Moon, J. (2008). Multinational corporation codes of conduct: governance tools for corporate social responsibility? **Corporate Governance,** 16 (4) pp. 294-311.

Borkowski, S. C., Welsh, M. J. & Wentzel, K. (2012). Sustainability reporting at Johnson & Johnson: A case study using content analysis, **International Journal of Business Insights & Transformation.** 4, pp 96-105.

Botosan, C. A. (1997). Disclosure level and the cost of equity capital. **The Accounting Review,** 72 (3) pp. 323–349.

Bouten, L., Everaet, P. and Roberts, P. W. (2012). How a Two-Step Approach Discloses Different Determinants of Voluntary Social and Environmental Reporting. **Journal of Business Finance & Accounting,** 39(5) & (6), pp. 567–605.

Bouten, L., P., Everaert, L., Van Liedekerke, L., De Moor and Christiaens, J. (2011) Corporate Social Responsibility Reporting: A Comprehensive Picture. **Accounting Forum,** 35(3) pp. 187–204.

Bowman, E. (1978). Strategy, annual reports, and alchemy. **California Management Review,** 20, pp. 64-71.

Boyatzis, R. (1998). **Transforming qualitative information: Thematic analysis and code development.** Thousand Oaks, California: Sage Publications.

Brammer, S.J. and Millington, A. I. (2005). Corporate Reputation and Philanthropy: An Empirical Analysis. **Journal of Business Ethics,** 61 (1) pp. 29–44.

Branco, M.C. and Rodrigues, L. L. (2008). Factors Influencing Social Responsibility Disclosure by Portuguese Companies. **Journal of Business Ethics,** 83 (4) December, pp. 685–701.

Brennann, L., Binney, W., McChrohan, J and Lancaster, N (2009). Implementation of environmental sustainability in business: Suggestions for improvement, Australasian Marketing Journal (AMJ), 19, pp. 52-57.

Brown, H.S., de Jong, M., Levy, D.L. (2009a). Building institutions based on information disclosure: lessons from GRI's sustainability reporting. **Journal of Cleaner Production** 17 (6) pp. 571-580.

Brown, J. and Fraser, M. (2006). Approaches and perspectives in social and environmental accounting: an overview of the conceptual landscape. **Business Strategy and the Environment,** 15 pp. 103-117.

Brown, N., and Deegan, C. (1998). The public disclosure of environmental performance information—a dual test of media agenda setting theory and legitimacy theory. **Accounting and business research,** 29(1), pp. 21-41.

Buhr, N. (2002). A structuration view on the initiation of environmental reports. **Critical Perspectives on Accounting,** 13, pp. 17-38.

Burgwal and Viera, (2014). Environmental Disclosure Determinants in Dutch Listed Companies. **R. Cont. Fin. – USP,** 25 (64), pp. 60-78,

Byrne, J., Martinez, C and Glover, L. (2002). "A brief on environmental justice. In Environmental justice: Discourses in international political economy", ed. J. Byrne, L. Glover, and C. Martinez, 3–17. New Brunswick, NJ, and London: Transaction Books.

Cahan, S.F. Rahman, A. and Perera H. (2005). Global diversification and corporate disclosure. **Journal of International Accounting Research,** 4 (1) pp. 73–93.

Camfferman, K, and Cooke, T.E. (2002). An analysis of disclosure in the annual reports of UK and Dutch companies, **Journal of International Accounting Research,** 1, (1), pp. 3-30.

Campbell, D (2004). A longitudinal and cross-sectional analysis of environmental disclosure in UK companies—a research note. The British Accounting Review, 36, pp. 107-117.

Campbell, D. J. (200) Legitimacy theory or managerial reality construction? Corporate social disclosure in Markd and Spencer Plc corporate reports, 1969-1997. **Accounting Forum,** 24(1), pp.1-21.

Campbell, D., Craven, B., and Shrives, P. (2003). Voluntary social reporting in three FTSE sectors: a comment on perception and legitimacy. **Accounting, Auditing and Accountability Journal,** 16 (4) pp. 558-581.

Campbell, J.L., (2007). Why would corporations behave in socially responsible ways? An institutional theory of corporate social responsibility. **Academy of Management Review** 32(3) pp. 946-967.

Carroll, A. and Buchholtz, A. (2006). **Business and society: Ethics and stakeholder management.** 6th ed. Mason, Ohio: Thompson South-Western.

Castka, P. and Balzarova, M. (2008). Social responsibility standardization: guidance or reinforcement through certification. **Human Systems Management,** 27 pp. 231-242.

Chandler, A. (1977). The visible hand. **Harvard University Press,** Cambridge, MA. Chapman and Hall.

Chau, G. and Gray, S. J. (2002). Ownership structure and corporate voluntary disclosure in Hong Kong and Singapore. **The International Journal of Accounting,** 37 (2) pp. 247–265.

Chau, G., and Gray, S. J. (2010). Family ownership, board independence and voluntary disclosure: Evidence from Hong Kong. **Journal of International Accounting, Auditing and Taxation,** 19(2), pp. 93-109.

Chavent, M., Ding, Y., Fu, L., Stolowy, H & Wang, H (2006). Disclosure and determinants studies: An extension using the Divisive Clustering Method (DIV). **European Accounting Review,** 15, pp. 181-218.

Chen, C.J.P. and Jaggi, B. (2000). Association between independent non-executive directors, family control and financial disclosures in Hong Kong. **Journal of Accounting and Public Policy,** 19 (4-5), pp. 285-310

Chenhall, R. H. and R. Juchau, R. (1977) Investor Information Needs—An Australian Study, **Accounting and Business Research,** 7 (26), pp. 111-119.

Cheung, W. K. A., & Wei, K.C.J. (2006). Insider ownership and corporate performance: Evidence from the adjustment cost approach. Journal of Corporate Finance, 12, p. 913.

Cho, C. H., and Patten, D. M. (2007). The role of environmental disclosures as tools of legitimacy: a research note. **Accounting, Organizations and Society,** 32 (7/8), pp. 639-647.

Christ, K. L., and Burritt, R. L. (2013). Environmental management accounting: the significance of contingent variables for adoption. **Journal of Cleaner Production,** 41, pp.163-173.

Clarkson, M. (1995). A stakeholder framework for analyzing and evaluating corporate social performance. **Academy of Management Review,** 20 (1) pp. 92-117.

Clarkson, P. M., Li, Y., Richardson, G. D., and Vasvari, F. P. (2008). Revisiting the relation between environmental performance and environmental disclosure: an empirical analysis. **Accounting, Organizations and Society**, 33 (4/5) pp. 303-327.

Clarkson, P. M., Li, Y., Richardson, G. D., and Vasvari, F. P. (2011). Does it really pay to be green? Determinants and consequences of proactive environmental strategies. **Journal of Accounting and Public Policy**, 30 (2) pp.122-144.

Clarkson, P.M., Li, Y., Richardson, G. D. and Vasvari, F.P. (2008). Revisiting the Relation Between Environmental Performance and Environmental Disclosure: An Empirical Analysis. **Accounting, Organizations and Society**, 33 (4and5), pp. 303–327.

Clatworthy, M & Jones, M.J. (2003). Financial reporting of good news and bad news: evidence from accounting narratives, Accounting and Business Research, 33, pp. 171-185.

Coase R.H (1937). The Nature of the Firm, Economica, 4, pp. 386–405

Cooke, T. E. (1989). Disclosure in the corporate annual reports of Swedish companies. **Accounting and Business Research,** 19 (74) pp.113-124.

Cooper, S. M. and Owen, D. L. (2007). Corporate social reporting and stakeholder accountability: The missing link. Accounting. **Organizations and Society**, 32, (7–8), pp. 649–667.

Cormier, D., and Magnan, M. (2003) Environmental reporting management: a continental European perspective. **Journal of Accounting and Public Policy,** 22 (1), pp. 43-62.

Cormier, D., Gordon, I. M. (2001). An examination of social and environmental reporting strategies, **Accounting, Auditing & Accountability Journal**, 14, pp.587-617.

Cormier, D., Gordon, I.M., and Magnan, M. (2004). Corporate Environmental Disclosure: Contrasting Management's Perceptions with Reality. **Journal of Business Ethics**, 49(2), 143–165.

Cormier, D., Magnan, M., and Van Velthoven, B. (2005). Environmental Disclosure Quality in Large German Companies: Economic Incentives, Public Pressures or Institutional Conditions? **European Accounting Review,** 14(1), pp. 3–39.

Cowen, S. S., Ferreri, L. B., and Parker, L. D. (1987). The impact of corporate characteristics on social responsibility: disclosure a typology and frequency-based analysis. **Accounting, Organizations and Society,** 12 (2) pp.111-122.

CSBR (2008). CSR Trends 2008. Our Second Comprehensive Survey of Sustainability Report Trends, Benchmarks and Best Practices, **Canadian Business for Social Responsibility and Craib Design and Communication**, Toronto.

Da Silva Monteiro, S. M. and Aibar-Guzman, B, (2010). Determinants of environmental disclosure in the annual reports of large companies operating in Portugal. **Corp. Soc. Responsib. Environ. Mgmt,** Vol 17, pp. 185–204.

Dainelli, F., Bini, L. and Giunta, F. (2013). Signalling strategies in annual reports: Evidence from the disclosure of performance indicators. **Advances in Accounting,** 29 (2) December, pp. 267–277.

Daub, C. H. (2007). Assessing the quality of sustainability reporting: an alternative methodological approach. **Journal of Cleaner Production,** 15 pp. 75-85.

Davidson, D. K. (1991). Legitimacy: how important is it for Tobacco strategies. **Business & the Contemporary World,** pp. 50-58.

Davis, G. and Searcy, C. (2010) A review of Canadian corporate sustainable development reports. **Journal of Global Responsibility** 1 (2) pp. 316-329.

Davis, K. (1973). The case for and against business assumption of social responsibilities. **Academy of Management Journal,** 16, pp. 312-322.

De Villiers, C.J. and Van Staden, C. J. (2006). Can less environmental disclosure have a legitimising effect? Evidence from Africa. **Accounting, Organizations and Society,** 31 (8) (2006), pp. 763–781.

Deegan C. and Gordon, B. (1996). A study of environmental disclosure practices of Australian Corporations. **Accounting and Business Research,** 26 (3) pp. 187-199.

Deegan C. and Rankin, M. (1996). Do Australian companies objectively report environmental news? An analysis of environmental disclosures by firms successfully prosecuted by the Environmental Protection Authority. **Accounting, Auditing and Accountability Journal,** 9 (2) pp. 50-67.

Deegan C. and Rankin, M. and Voght, P. (2000) Firm's disclosure reactions to major social incidents: Australian evidence. Accounting Forum. 24 (1) pp. 101-130.

Deegan, C. & Carrol G (1993). An Analysis of Incentives for Australian Firms to Apply for Reporting Excellence Awards. Accounting and Business Research Vol. 23, pp. 219-227.

Deegan, C. (2000). **Financial accounting theory.** New South Wales: McGraw Hill. p. 343

Deegan, C. (2002) Introduction: The Legitimising Effect of Social and Environmental Disclosures – A Theoretical Foundation. **Accounting, Auditing and Accountability Journal,** 15 (3) pp. 282–311.

Deegan, C. (2002). "Introduction: The legitimizing effect of social and environmental disclosures – a theoretical foundation", **Accounting, Auditing & Accountability Journal**, Vol. 15 (3), pp. 282-311

Deegan, C. and Gordon, B. (1996). A study of the environmental disclosure practices of Australian corporations. **Accounting and Business Research**, 26 (3) pp. 187-199.

Deegan, C. and Hallam, A. (1991). The voluntary ptrsentation of value added statement in Australia: A political cost perspective, **Accounting & Finance**, 31 (1), pp.1–21.

Deegan, C. and Unerman, J. (2006). **Financial Accounting Theory**, UK: McGraw-Hill.

Deegan, C. and Unerman, J. (2008). Financial accounting theory: European edition. Maidenhead, Berkshire: McGraw-Hill Education. (Originally published 2006).

Deegan, C., and Gordon, B. (1996). A study of the environmental disclosure practices of Australian corporations. **Accounting and Business Research**, 26 (3), pp.187-199.

Deegan, C., and Rankin, M. (1996). Do Australian companies report environmental news objectively? An analysis of environmental disclosures by firms prosecuted successfully by the Environmental Protection Authority. **Accounting, auditing & accountability journal**, 9(2), pp. 50-67.

Deegan, C., Rankin, M. and Voght, P. (2000). Firms' disclosure reactions to major social incidents: Australian evidence. **Accounting Forum**, 24 (1) pp. 101-130.

Deegan, C., Rankin, M., and Tobin, J. (2002) An examination of the corporate social and environmental disclosures of BHP from 1983-1997: a test of legitimacy theory. **Accounting, Auditing and Accountability Journal**, 15 (3), pp. 312-343.

Depoers, F. (2000). A cost-benefit study of voluntary disclosure: Some empirical evidence from French listed companies. **The European Accounting Review**, 9(2), pp. 245-263.

DesJardins, J. (1998). Corporate environmental responsibility. Journal of Business Ethics, 17(8), pp. 825-838.

Dierkes M. and Antal, A. B. (1985). The Usefulness and Use of Social reporting Information. **Accounting, Organization and Society**, 10 (1) pp. 29-34.

Donaldson T. and Preston, L. E. (1995). The Stakeholder Theory of The Corporation: Concepts, Evidence, and Implications P. **Academy of Management Review**, 20 (1) pp. 65-91.

Donaldson, T (1989). The Ethics of International Business, New York: Oxford University Press

Dong, Y. M., Ishikawa, Liu, X., and Hamori, S. (2011). The determinants of citizen complaints on environmental pollution: an empirical study from China. **Journal of Cleaner Production,** 19 (12), pp. 1306-1314.

Dow Jones Sustainability Index (DJSI) (2011). Dow Jones Sustainability Indexes [Online]. Availablefrom:http://www.sustainability-index.com/djsi_protected/djsi_na/ SAM_DJSINA_Components.pdf (Accessed June 21, 2011).

Dowling, J., and Pfeffer, J. (1975). Organizational legitimacy: Social values and organizational behavior. **Pacific sociological review,** pp. 122-136.

Drucker, P. (1946). **Concept of the Corporation.** New York: John Day.

Drucker, P. F. (1984). The discipline of innovation. **Harvard business review,** 63(3), pp. 67-72.

Dyllick, T. and Hockerts, K. (2002). Beyond the business case for corporate sustainability. **Business Strategy and the Environment,** 11 pp. 130-141.

Eccles, R. (2012). Get Ready: Mandated Integrated Reporting is the Future of Corporate Reporting. **MIT Sloan Management Review,** March, pp. 1-5.

Elijido-Ten, E., Kloot, L., and Clarkson, P. (2010). Extending the application of stakeholder influence strategies to environmental disclosures: An exploratory study from a developing country. **Accounting, Auditing & Accountability Journal,** 23(8), pp. 1032-1059.

Elkington J. (1999). Cannibals with Forks-The Triple Bottom Line of 21st Century Business, Capstone. **Employee Communication and Consultation, Advisory Booklet,** acas - 1996.

Elkington, J. (1998). **Cannibals with Forks: The Triple Bottom Line of 21st Century Business.** New Society Publishers, Stony Creek, CT.

Eng, L.L. and Mak, Y. T. (2003). Corporate governance and voluntary disclosure. **Journal of Accounting and Public Policy,** 22 pp. 325–345

Epstein, M. J. and Freedman, M., (1994). "Social Disclosure and The Individual Investor", **Accounting, Auditing & Accountability Journal,** 7(4), pp. 94-109.

Erlandsson, J., and Tillman, A.-M. (2009). Analysing influencing factors of corporate environmental information collection, management and communication. **Journal of Cleaner Production,** 17 (9), pp. 800-810.

Evan, W. M. and Freeman, R. E. (1993). "A Stakeholder Theory of Modern Corporation: Kantian Capitalism". In Beauchamp and Bowie, Ethical Theory and Business, Prentice Hall.

Farneti, F. and Siboni, B. (2011). An analysis of the Italian governmental guidelines and of the local governments' practices for social reports. **Sustainability Accounting, Management and Policy Journal**, 2, pp. 101-125.

Farneti, F., and Guthrie, J. (2009, June). Sustainability reporting by Australian public sector organisations: Why they report. **In Accounting forum**, 33 (2), pp. 89-98.

Firth, M. (1978). Qualified Audit Reports: Their Impact on Investment Decisions. **The Accounting Review,** 53(3), pp. 642-650.

Firth, M. (1984). The extent of voluntary disclosure in corporate annual reports and its association with security risk measures. **Applied Economics Volume**, 16 (2), Pp. 269-278.

Fortanier, F., Kolk, A. and Pinkse, J. Manag (2011). Harmonization in CSR Reporting, Management international review 51: 665.

Francoeur, C., Labelle, R. & Sinclair-Desgagné, B. (2008) Gender Diversity in Corporate Governance and Top Management. **J Bus Ethics,** Vol 81, p. 88

Freedman, M. and Jaggi B. (1986). An Analysis of the Impact of Corporate Pollution Disclosures Included in Annual Financial Statements on Investment Decisions. **Advances in Public Interest Accounting**, pp. 193–212

Freedman, M., and Jaggi, B. (1982). Pollution disclosures, pollution performance and economic performance. **Omega**, 10 (2), pp. 167-176.

Freedman, M., and Jaggi, B. (1988). An analysis of the association between pollution disclosure and economic performance. **Accounting, Auditing and Accountability Journal**, 1 (2), pp. 43-58.

Freeman, R. E. (1984). **Strategic management: A stakeholder approach**. Boston: Pitman Publishing.

Freeman, R., Harrison, J., Wicks, A., Parmar, B., and De Colle, S. (2010). **Stakeholder theory: the state of the art**. Cambridge: Cambridge University Press. p. 344.

Frost, G. and Semaer, M. (2002). Adoption of environmental reporting and management practices: an analysis of New South Wales public sector entities. **Financial Accountability and Management,** 18 pp. 103-127.

Gallego, I. (2006). The use of economic, social and environmental indicators as a measure of sustainable development in Spain. **Corporate Social Responsibility and Environmental Management** 13 pp. 78-97.

Gallo, P.J. and Christensen, L.J. (2011) "Firm Size Matters: An Empirical Investigation of Organizational Size and Ownership on Sustainability-Related Behaviors", Business and Society, Vol 50

Gamerschlag, R., Moller, K. and Verbeeten F. (2011). Determinants of voluntary CSR disclosure: Empirical evidence from Germany. **Review of Managerial Science,** 5 (2–3) pp. 233–262.

Gao, S. S., Heravi, S. and Xiao, J. Z. (2005). Determinants of corporate social and environmental reporting in Hong Kong: a research note. **Accounting Forum.** Vol 29. pp. 233-242.

García-Sánchez, I., Frías-Aceituno, J. and Luis Rodríguez-Domínguez, L. (2013). Determinants of corporate social disclosure in Spanish local governments. **Journal of Cleaner Production,** 39 pp. 60-72.

Garsombke, H. (1979). The relationship between corporate disclosure and firm risk. **Journal of Business Finance & Accounting,** 6(1), pp. 53-70.

Ghana Stock Exchange Fact Book, Ghana Stock Exchange Publication, Accra (2009)

Ghana Stock Exchange Publication, Accra (2007), Ghana Stock Exchange Fact Book, 1990

Ghazali, N.M.A., and Wheetman, P (2006). "Perpetuating traditional influences: Voluntary disclosure in Malaysia following the economic crisis", **Journal of International Accounting, Auditing and Taxation,** Vol 15

Ghazoli, I (2007). The Application of the Multivariate analysis by using SPSS Program, Semarang: Publishing Board of UNDIP

Gill, J. and Johnson, P. (1991). **Research Methods for Managers**. Paul Chapman Publishing Ltd., London.

Gladwin, T.N., Kennelly, J.J. and Krause, T. S. (1995). Shifting paradigms for sustainable development: implications for management theory and research. **Academy of Management Review,** 20 (4) pp. 874-907.

Glaum, M. and Street, D. (2003). Compliance with the Disclosure Requirement of German's New Market, IAS Versus US GAAP". **Journal of International Financial Management and Accounting,** 14(1), pp. 64-100.

Global Reporting Initiative (2009). About GRI. Retrieved from http://www.globalreporting.org/AboutGRI.

Global Reporting Initiative (GRI), (2006) Sustainability Reporting Guidelines Version 3.0. GRI, Amsterdam.

Global Reporting Initiative (GRI), (2010) Sustainability Reporting Guidelines Version 3.0. GRI, Amsterdam.

Global Reporting Initiative (GRI), (2011a) What is GRI? Available from: http://www. globalreporting.org/AboutGRI/WhatIsGRI/ [Accessed June 17, 2011].

Global Reporting Initiative (GRI), (2011b) Sustainability Reporting Guidelines: Version 3.1. GRI, Amsterdam.

Gonella C., Pilling, A. and S. Zadek (1998). Making Values Counts: Contemporary Experience in Social and Ethical **Accounting, Auditing and Reporting**. ACCA Research Report 57.

Gray F. (1992). Accounting and Environmentalism: An Exploration of The Challenge of Gently Accounting For Accountability, Transparency and Sustainability. **Accounting, Organization and Society**, 17 (5) pp. 399-425.

Gray R., Javad, M., Power, D. M. and Sinclair, D. (1999). Social and Environmental Disclosure and Corporate Characteristics: A research note and extension, Discussion Paper, University of Dundee, June.

Gray R., Kouhy, I. and Lavers, S. (1995b). Constructing a research database of social and environmental reporting by UK companies: a methodological note. **Accounting, Auditing and Accountability**, 8 (2) June, pp. 78-101

Gray R., Kouhy, R and Lavers, S. (1995a). Corporate social and environmental reporting: a review of the literature and a longitudinal study of UK disclosure. **Accounting, Auditing and Accountability**, 8 (2) June, pp. 47-77

Gray R., Owen, D and Maunders, K. (1987). **Corporate Social Reporting: Accounting and accountability**, Hemel Hempstead: Prentice Hall.

Gray R., Owen, D. and Adams, C. (1996). **Accounting and Accountability - changes and Challenges in corporate social and environmental reporting**. Prentice Hall.

Gray R., Owen, D. and Maunders, K. (1988). Corporate Social Reporting: Emerging Trends in Accountability and The Social Contract. **Accounting, Auditing and Accountability**, pp. 6-20.

Gray R., Owen, D. and Maunders, K. (1991). Accountability, Corporate Social Reporting, and the External Social Audits. **Advances in Public Interest Accounting**, 4 pp. 1-21.

Gray, R. (2010). Is accounting for sustainability actually accounting for sustainability and how would we know? An exploration of narratives of organisations and the planet. **Accounting, Organizations and Society,** 35 pp. 47-62.

Gray, R. H., M. Javad, D.M. Power and C.D. Sinclair (2001). "Social and environmental disclosure and corporate characteristics: A research note and extension" **Journal of Business Finance and Accounting.** 28.3/4, April/May pp 327-356.

Gray, R., Dey, C., Owen, D., Evans, R., and Zadek, S. (1997). Struggling with the praxis of social accounting: Stakeholders, accountability, audits and procedures. **Accounting, Auditing and Accountability Journal,** 10 (3) pp. 325-364.

Gray, R., Kouhy, R., and Lavers, S. (1995). Corporate social and environmental reporting: a review of the literature and a longitudinal study of UK disclosure. **Accounting, Auditing and Accountability Journal,** 8 (2), pp. 47-77.

Gray, R., Kouhy, R., and Lavers, S. (1995). Methodological themes: Constructing a research database of social and environmental reporting by UK companies. **Accounting, Auditing and Accountability Journal,** 8 (2) pp. 78-101.

Gray, R., Owen, D., and Adams, C. (1996). **Accounting and accountability: Changes and challenges in corporate social and environmental reporting.** London: Prentice-Hall.

Gray, R., R. Kouhy and S. Lavers (1995a). Corporate Social and Environmental Reporting: A Review of the Literature and a Longitudinal Study of UK Disclosure. **Accounting, Auditing and Accountability Journal,** 8 (2) pp. 47–77.

Griffin, J. J., and Mahon, J. F. (1997). The corporate social performance and corporate financial performance debate twenty-five years of incomparable research. **Business & Society,** 36(1), pp. 5-31.

GTZ (2009). Corporate Social Responsibility in sub-Saharan Africa: A survey on Promoting and Hindering Factors.

Gul, F. A., and Leung, S. (2004). Board leadership, outside directors' expertise and voluntary corporate disclosures. **Journal of Accounting and public Policy,** 23(5), pp. 351-379.

Gurvitsh, N & Sidorova, I (2012). Survey of Sustainability Reporting Integrated into Annual Reports of Estonian Companies for the years 2007-2010: Based on Companies Listed on Tallinn Stock Exchange as of October 2011, Procedia Economics and Finance, Vol 2, pp. 26-34.

Guthrie J, Dumay J and Farneti F (2010). GRI Sustainability Reporting Guidelines For Public And Third Sector Organizations: **Public Management Review.** Vol. 12 pp. 531-548.

Guthrie J. and Parker, L. D. (1989). Corporate Social Reporting: A Rebuttal of Legitimacy Theory. **Accounting and Business Research** 19 (76) pp. 343-352.

Guthrie J. and Parker, L. D. (1990). Corporate Social Disclosure Practice: A Comparative International Analysis. **Advances in Public Interest Accounting,** 3 pp. 159-175.

Guthrie, J. Cuganesan, S. and Ward, L (2008). Disclosure media for social and environmental matters within the Australian food and beverage industry. **Social and Environmental Accountability Journal,** 28 (1), pp. 33-44.

Guthrie, J.and Abeysekera, I. (2006). Content analysis of social, environmental reporting: What is new? **Journal of Human Resource Costing and Accounting,** 10 (2), pp. 114–126.

Hackston D. and Milne, M. (1996). Some determinants of social and environmental disclosure in New Zealand companies, **Accounting, Auditing and Accountability Journal,** 9 (1) pp. 77-108.

Hackston, D. and Milne, M.J. (1996). Some determinants of social and environmental disclosures in New Zealand companies, Accounting, Auditing & Accountability Journal, Vol. 9.

Hahn, R. and Kühnen, M. (2013). Determinants of sustainability reporting: a review of results, trends, theory, and opportunities in an expanding field of research. **Journal of Cleaner Production,** 59 pp. 5-21.

Halme, M & Huse, M (1997). The influence of corporate governance, industry and country factors on environmental reporting, Scandinavian Journal of Management, Vol 13, pp. 137-157.

Hancock, P. (1993). Green and Gold-Sustaining Mineral Wealth, Australians and their Environment. **Centre for Resource and Environmental Studies,** Australian National University, Canberra, ACT p. 288.

Hanffa, R & Hudaib, M (2006). Corporate Governance Structure and Performance of Malaysian Listed Companies. **Journal of Business Finance and Accounting,** Vol 13, pp 1048, pp. 1050-1051.

Haniffa R.M., and Cooke T.E. (2005). The impact of culture and governance on corporate social reporting. Journal of Accounting and Public Policy, Vol 24, pp. 391-430.

Haniffa, R. M. and Cooke, T. E. (2002). Culture, corporate governance and disclosure in Malaysian corporations. **Abacus,** 38(3), pp. 317-349.

Harrison J.S. and Freeman, I. E. (1999). Stakeholders, Social Responsibility, Empirical Evidence and Theoretical Perspectives. **Academy of Management Journal**, 42 (5) pp. 479-485.

Harte G. and Owen, D. (1991). Environmental Disclosure in the Annual reports of British Companies: A Research Note. **Accounting, Auditing and Accountability Journal**, 4 (3) pp. 51-61.

Hayes, A. F., and Krippendorff, K. (2007). Answering the call for a standard reliability measure for coding data. **Communication methods and measures**, 1(1), pp. 77-89.

Hedberg, C. J., von Malmborg, F. (2003). The Global Reporting Initiative and corporate sustainability reporting in Swedish companies. **Corporate Social Responsibility and Environmental Management**, 10, pp. 153-164.

Hilson G., and Basu, A.J. (2003). Devising indicators of sustainable development for the mining and minerals industry: An analysis of critical background issues, International Journal of Sustainable Development & World Ecology 10, pp. 319-331.

Hinson, R, Boateng R, Madichie N, (2010). Corporate social responsibility activity reportage on bank websites in Ghana. **International Journal of Bank Marketing**, 28(7), pp.498-518.

Hinson, R., Boateng, R. and Madichie, N. (2010). Corporate social responsibility activity reportage on bank websites in Ghana. **International Journal of Bank Marketing**, 28 (7), pp. 498-518.

Ho, L.C.J. and Taylor M.E. (2007). An Empirical Analysis of Triple Bottom-Line Reporting and its Determinants: Evidence from the United States and Japan, **Journal of international Financial Management and Accounting,** Vol 18

Ho, S. S. M. Wong, K. S. (2001). A study of the relationship between corporate governance structures and the extent of voluntary disclosure. **Journal of International Accounting, Auditing and Taxation**, 10 pp. 139–156.

Hogner, R. H, (1982). "Corporate social reporting: eight decades of development at US Steel", Research in Corporate Performance and Policy

Holthausen, R. W., and Leftwich, R. W. (1983). The economic consequences of accounting choice implications of costly contracting and monitoring. **Journal of Accounting and Economics,** 5, pp. 77-117.

Honger R H (1982). Corporate Social Reporting; Eight years of Development at US Steel. **Research in Corporate Performance and Policy**, pp.243-250.

Hooghiemstra, R. (2000). Corporate communication and impression management- New perspectives why companies engage in Corporate social Reporting. **Journal of business ethics,** 27 pp. 55-68.

Hopwood A.G (2009). Accounting and the Environment. Accounting, Organizations and Society, 34, pp. 433-439.

Hossain, M and Reaz, M (2007). Corporate governance around the world: An investigation, Journal of American Academy of Business, Cambridge

Hossain, M and Reaz, M (2007). The determinants and characteristics of voluntary disclosure by Indian banking companies, **Corporate Social Responsibility and Environmental Management**, Vol 14, Issue 5, pp. 274–288.

Hossain, M. and Hammami, H (2009) Voluntary disclosure in the annual reports of an emerging country: The case of Qatar. **Advances in Accounting, incorporating Advances in International Accounting,** 25, pp. 255–265.

Huang, C. L., and Kung, F. H. (2010). Drivers of environmental disclosure and stakeholder expectation: Evidence from Taiwan. **Journal of Business Ethics**, 96(3), pp. 435-451.

Hubbard, G. (2009) Measuring organizational performance: beyond the triple bottom line. **Business Strategy and the Environment**, 19, pp.177-191.

Hughes, S. B., Anderson, A., and Golden, S. (2001) Corporate environmental disclosures: are they useful in determining environmental performance? **Journal of Accounting and Public Policy**, 20 (3), pp. 217-240.

Hussey J. and Hussey, R (1996) Business research A Practical Guide for Undergraduate and Postgraduate Students. Macmillan Business.

Hussey, J. and Hussey, R. (1997), **Business Research**, Macmillan Press Ltd, Basingstoke

Idowu, S. O. and Towler, B. O. (2004) A comparative study of the contents of corporate social responsibility reports of UK companies, Management of Environmental Quality. **An International Journal,** 15 (4), pp.420 – 437.

IFAC, 2006, IFAC. International Federation of Accountants' handbook of international auditing, assurance, and ethics pronouncements (2006)

IISD (International Institute for Sustainable Development). 1992. Trade and sustainable development. Winnipeg, Manitoba.

Isaksson, R., and Steimle, U. (2009) What does GRI-reporting tell us about corporate sustainability? **The TQM Journal**, 21(2), pp. 168-181.

Islam, M.Z., and Deegan, C. (2008). Motivations for an organization within a developing country to report social responsibility information: Evidence from Bangladesh, **Accounting, Auditing & Accountability Journal,** 21(6), pp.850-874.

Jamali D, Safieddine A.M and Rabbath M (2008). Corporate Governance and Corporate Social Responsibility Synergies and Interrelationships. Corporate Governance: An International Review.

Jenkins, H. (2004). Corporate social responsibility and the mining industry: conflicts and constructs. **Corporate Social Responsibility and Environmental Management,** 11(1), pp. 23-34.

Jensen, M.C. and W.H. Meckling, (1976). Theory of the firm: managerial behavior, agency costs, and ownership structure. **Journal of Financial Economics,** 3, pp. 305–360.

Johnson, T & Gjoelberg, O (2009) Management of the Norwegian oil fund: The challenges and costs of being ethical. Scandinavian Journal of Business Research,

Jose, A. and Lee, S.M. (2007). Environmental Reporting of Global Corporations: A Content Analysis based on Website Disclosures, **J Bus Ethics** 72, p. 307.

Joseph, C. and Taplin, R. (2011). The Measurement of Sustainability Disclosure: Abundance versus Occurrence. **Accounting Forum,** 35 (1) pp. 19–31.

Joseph, G. (2012) Ambiguous but tethered: An accounting basis for sustainability Reporting. **Critical Perspectives on Accounting,** 23 pp. 93– 106.

Kemp, R. (2001) Environmental Policy and Technological Change: A Comparison of Technological Impact of Policy Instruments.

Khalid, S. M, Hennell, A, and Solomon, J. (2013) Site-specific and geographical segmental social, environmental and ethical disclosures by the mining sector. Unpublished manuscripts.

Kisenyi, V. and Gray, R. H. (1998). Social disclosure in Uganda. **Social and Environmental Accounting,** 18 (2), pp. 16-18.

Kolk, A. (2003). Trends in sustainability reporting by the fortune global 250. **Business Strategy and the Environment,** 12 (5), pp. 279-291.

Kolk, A., and Perego, P. (2010) Determinants of the adoption of sustainability assurance statements: an international investigation. **Business Strategy and the Environment,** 19 (3), pp.182-198.

Kothari, S.P. and Collins, J. W. (1989) An analysis of inter-temporal and cross-sectional determinants of Earning Response Coefficients. **Journal of Accounting and Economics,** 11 pp.143-181.

Krippendorff, K. (1980) **Content analysis: an introduction to its methodology.** London: Sage.

Krippendorff, K. (2004) **Content analysis: An introduction to its methodology.** 2nd ed. Thousand Oaks, California: Sage Publications.

Kuasirikun, N., and Sherer, M. (2004). Corporate social accounting disclosure in Thailand. **Accounting, Auditing & Accountability Journal,** 17(4), pp. 629-660.

Kumah, A. (2006) Sustainability and gold mining the developing world. **Journal of Cleaner Production,** 14 (3–4), pp. 315–323.

La Porta R, López-de-Silanes F, and Shleifer A. (1999). Corporate ownership around the world. The Journal of Finance LIV, pp. 471–517.

Lamberton 920050 Sustainability accounting—A brief history and conceptual framework. **Accounting Forum,** 29 (1), pp. 7–26.

Lamprinidi, S. and Kubo, N. (2008) Debate: the global reporting initiative and public agencies. **Public Money and Management** 28, pp. 326-329.

Lang, M., & Lundholm, R. (1993). Cross-Sectional Determinants of Analyst Ratings of Corporate Disclosures. **Journal of Accounting Research,** 31(2), 246-271.

Langer, M. (2006) **Comparability of sustainability reports. A comparative content analysis of Austrian sustainability reports.** Quoted in: Schaltegger, S., Bennett, M.,

Leeson, R. and Ivers, J. (2005) Sustainability reporting by the public sector: momentum changes in the practice, Uptake and form of reporting by public agencies. **Accountability Forum** 8, pp. 12-21.

Leftwich, R.W., Watts, R. L. and Zimmerman, J. L. (1981) Voluntary corporate disclosure: the case of interim reporting. **Journal of Accounting Research,** (Studies on Standardization of Accounting Practices: An Assessment of Alternative Institutional Arrangements). 19, pp. 50-77.

Lemon, A. J. and Cahan, S. F. (1997) Environmental Legislation and Environmental Disclosures: Some Evidence From New Zealand. **Asian Review of Accounting,** 5 (1) pp. 78 – 105.

L'Etang, J. (1995). Ethical corporate social responsibility: A framework for managers. **Journal of Business Ethics,** 14(2), pp. 125-132.

Leventis, S., and Weetman, P. (2004) Timeliness of financial reporting: applicability of disclosure theories in an emerging capital market. **Accounting and Business Research,** 34(1), pp. 43-56.

Li, Y., Clackson, P.M., Richardson, G.D. & Vasvari, F.P. (2008) Revisiting the relation between environmental performance and environmental disclosure: An empirical analysis. **Accounting, Organizations and Society,** 33 (4–5), pp. 303-327.

Lim, S. and McKinnon, J. (1993) Voluntary disclosure by NSW statutory authorities: The influence of political visibility. **Journal of Accounting and Public Policy,** 12 (3), pp. 189–216.

Lim, S., Matolcsy, Z. and Chow, D. (2007). The association between board composition and different types of voluntary disclosure. **The European Accounting Review,** 16 (3) pp. 555–583.

Lindblom C. E. (1984). The accountability of the private enterprise: private enterprise: private-no. Enterprise–yes. Quoted in Tinker A. M. (ed.), Social accounting for Corporations, Marcus Weiner, New York.

Lindblom C. K. (1994). The Concept of Organizational Legitimacy and its Implications for Corporate Social Responsibility Disclosure, paper presented at the Critical Perspectives on Accounting Conference, New York.

Lindblom, C. K. (2010). The implications of organisational legitimacy for corporate social performance and disclosure. Quoted in R. Gray, J. Bebbington, and S. Gray (Eds.), **Social and Environmental Accounting,** pp. 51-62. London: Sage Publications.

Liu, X., and Anbumozhi, V. (2009) Determinant factors of corporate environmental information disclosure: an empirical study of Chinese listed companies. **Journal of Cleaner Production,** 17 (6), pp. 593-600.

Lodhia, S. K. (2000). Social and environmental reporting in Fiji: A review of recent corporate annual reports. **Social and Environmental Accountability Journal,** 20(1), pp.15-18.

Lourenço, I. C. and Branco, M.C. (2013). Determinants of corporate sustainability performance in emerging markets: the Brazilian case. **Journal of Cleaner Production,** 57 pp. 134-141.

Lozano, R. and Huisingh, D. (2011). Inter-linking issues and dimensions in sustainability reporting. **Journal of Cleaner Production,** 19, (2–3), pp. 99–107.

Lu, Y and Abeysekera, I (2014). Stakeholders' power, corporate characteristics, and social and environmental disclosure: evidence from China, **Journal of Cleaner Production,** 64, pp. 426-436.

Mahadeoa, J. D., Oogarah-Hanumana, V. and Soobaroyenb, T. (2011) Changes in social and environmental reporting practices in an emerging economy (2004–2007): Exploring the relevance of stakeholder and legitimacy theories. **Accounting Forum,** 35 pp. 158– 175.

Malone, D., Fries, C and Jones, T (1993). An Empirical Investigation of the Extent of Corporate Financial Disclosure in the Oil and Gas Industry, **Journal of Accounting, Auditing & Finance,** Vol 8

Marcuccio, M. and Steccolini, I. (2005). Social and environmental reporting in local governments: a new Italian fashion? **Public Management Review,** 7 pp. 155-176.

Margolis, J. D., Elfenbein, H. A., and Walsh, J. P. (2007). Does it pay to be good? A meta-analysis and redirection of research on the relationship between corporate social and financial performance. **Ann Arbor,** 1001, pp. 48109-1234.

Mathews M. R. (1993). **Socially Responsible Accounting.** Chapman and Hall: London.

Mathews, M.R. (1987) Social and environmental accounting: A practical demonstration of ethical concern? J Bus Ethics 14, p. 663. Kluwer Academic Publishers

Maurer, J. G. (1971). **Readings in organization theory: Open-system approaches.** Random House (NY).

McGuire J. B., Schneeweis, T. and Hill, J. (1986) An analysis of alternative measures of strategic performance Quoted in R. Lamb and Stravastava. (Eds.) Advances in Strategic management, 4, pp. 107-153.

McMurtrie, T. (2005) Factors influencing the publication of social performance information: an Australian case study. **Corporate Social Responsibility and Environmental Management,** 12 (3), pp. 129-143.

McNally, G. M., Eng, L. H. and Hasseldine, C. R. (1982). Corporate financial reporting in New Zealand: An analysis of user preferences, corporate characteristics and disclosure practices for discretionary information. **Accounting and Business Research,** 13 pp. 11-20.

Meek GK, Roberts CB, and Gray AJ (1995). Factors influencing voluntary annual report disclosures by US, UK and continental European multinational corporations. **International Business Studies** 26(3), pp. 555–572.

Miller, P. (1991). Accounting innovation beyond the enterprise: problemizing investment decisions and programming economic growth in the UK in the 1960s. **Accounting, Organization and Society,** 16 (8), pp. 733-762.

Milne M. J. and Adler, R. W. (1999). Exploring the Reliability of Social and Environmental disclosures Content Analysis. **Accounting, Auditing and accountability Journal,** 12 (2) pp. 237-256.

Milne, M. J. (2002). Positive accounting theory, political costs and social disclosure analyses: a critical look. **Critical Perspectives on Accounting.** 13, pp. 369-395.

Milne, M. J. and Chan, C. C. (1999). NARRATIVE CORPORATE SOCIAL DISCLOSURES: HOW MUCH OF A DIFFERENCE DO THEY MAKE TO INVESTMENT DECISION-MAKING? **The British Accounting Review,** 31 (4), pp. 439–457.

Milne, M. J., and Patten, D. M. (2002). Securing organizational legitimacy. an experimental decision case examining the impact of environmental disclosures. **Accounting, Auditing and Accountability Journal,** 15 (3), pp. 372-405.

Minerals Commission and Chamber of Mines. Proceedings of National Mining Conference on Corporate Social Responsibility in Ghana, 2004. [Online] http://www.mincomgh.org/minerals_sector/index.html.

Mitchell, R.K., Agle, B.R. and Wood, D.J. (1997). Towards a theory of stakeholder identification and salience: defining the principle of who and what really counts. **Academy of Management Review,** 22 (4) pp. 853-886.

Mobus, J.L (2005). Mandatory environmental disclosures in a legitimacy theory context, **Accounting, Auditing & Accountability Journal,** 18 (4), pp.492-517.

Modi, S. (2012) A Study on the Adequacy and Efficacy of Working Capital in Automobile

Moneva, J. M., Archel, P. and Correa, C. (2006). GRI and the camouflaging of corporate unsustainability. **Accounting Forum,** 30, pp. 121-137.

Morhardt, J. E., Baird, S., and Freeman, K. (2002). Scoring corporate environmental and sustainability reports using GRI 2000, ISO 14031 and other criteria. **Corporate Social Responsibility and Environmental Management,** 9(4), pp. 215-233.

Mulgan, R. (2000). Accountability: an ever-expanding concept? **Public Administration,** 78 (3) pp. 555-573.

Murray, A., Sinclair, D., Power, D., and Gray, R. (2006) Do financial markets care about social and environmental disclosure? Further evidence and exploration from the UK. **Accounting, Auditing and Accountability Journal,** 19 (2), pp. 228-255.

Mussari, R and Monfardini, P. (2010). Practices of Social Reporting in Public Sector and Non-profit Organizations. **Public Management Review,** 12(4), pp. 487-492.

Nachmias C. F. and Nachmias, D. (1996). **Research Method in the Social Sciences.** 5th ed. Lodon: Arnold - Hodder Headline Group.

Navarro, A., Alcaraz, F.J., and Zafra, J. L. (2010). Disclosure of information on corporate responsibility in public administration: an empirical study in local governments. **Accounting Review,** 13, pp. 285-314.

Ness, K. E. and Mirza, A. M. (1991). Corporate social disclosure: A note on a test of agency theory. **The British Accounting Review**, 23 (3), pp. 211–217.

Neu, D., Warsame, H. and Pedwell, K. (1998). Managing public impressions: environmental disclosures in annual reports. **Accounting, Organizations and Society**, 23 (3) (1998), pp. 265–282.

Neuendorf, K. (2002) **The content analysis guidebook**. Thousand Oaks, California: Sage Publications.

Newson, M., and Deegan, C. (2002). Global expectations and their association with corporate social disclosure practices in Australia, Singapore, and South Korea. **The International Journal of Accounting**, 37(2), pp. 183-213.

O'Donovan, G. (2002) Environmental disclosures in the annual report: extending the applicability and predictive power of legitimacy theory. **Accounting, Auditing and Accountability Journal**, 15 (3), pp. 344-371.

O'Dwyer, B., Unerman, J. and Hession, E. (2005) User needs in sustainability reporting: Perspectives of stakeholders in Ireland. **European Accounting Review**, 14 (4) pp. 759-787.

Ofori, D. F. and Hinson, R. E. (2007). Corporate social responsibility (CSR) perspectives of leading firms in Ghana, Corporate Governance: **The international journal of business in society**, 7 (2), pp.178 – 193.

Orlitzky, M., Schmidt, F.L. and Rynes, S. L. (2003). Corporate Social and Financial Performance: A Meta-Analysis, Organization Studies, 24 (3), pp. 403-441.

Owen, D. (2008). Chronicles of wasted time?: A personal reflection on the current state of, and future prospects for, social and environmental accounting research, **Accounting, Auditing & Accountability Journal**, 21 (2), pp.240-267.

Owusu-Ansah, S. (1998). The impact of corporate attributes on the extent of mandatory disclosure and reporting by listed companies in Zimbabwe. **International Journal of Accounting**, 33(5), pp. 605-631.

Owusu-Ansah, S. (2000). Noncompliance with corporate annual report disclosure requirements in Zimbabwe. **Research in Accounting in Emerging Economies**, (4), pp. 289-305.

Oyelere P, Lasward F, and Fisher R. (2003). Determinants of Internet financial teporting by New Zealand companies. **Journal of International Financial. Management and Accounting** 14(1), pp.26–63.

Padgett, R.C. and Galan, J.I. (2010). The effect of R&D intensity on corporate social responsibility. **Journal of Business Ethics**, 93 pp. 407-418.

Panchapakesan, S. and McKinnon, J. (1992). Proxies for political visibility: a preliminary examination of the relation among some potential proxies. Accounting Research Journal.

Parker, L. D. (2005). Social and environmental accountability research: a view from the commentary box. **Accounting, Auditing & Accountability Journal**, 18(6), pp. 842-860.

Parsa, S and Kouhy R (2001). Disclosure of social information by UK companies: a case of legitimacy theory. Business and Economics Society International.

Parsa, S. & Kouhy, R. (2008). Social Reporting by Companies Listed on the Alternative Investment Market. **J Bus Ethics**, 79, p. 345.

Patelli, L. Prencipe, A. (2007). The relationship between voluntary disclosure and independent directors in the presence of a dominant shareholder. **The European Accounting Review**, 16 (1) pp. 5–33.

Patten D. M. (1992) Intra-industry environmental disclosures in response to the Alaskan oil spill: a note on legitimacy theory. **Accounting, Organizations and Society**, 17 (5) pp. 471- 475.

Patten, D. M. (1991). Exposure, legitimacy, and social disclosure. **Journal of Accounting and Public Policy**, 10 (4), pp. 297-308.

Patten, D. M. (2002). The relation between environmental performance and environmental disclosure: a research note. **Accounting, Organizations and Society**, 27 (8), pp. 763-773.

Patton, J. and Zelenka, I. (1997) An empirical analysis of the determinants of the extent of disclosure in annual reports of joint stock companies in the Czech Republic. **European Accounting Review Volume** 6, (4), pp. 605-626.

Phillips, R. A. (1997). Stakeholder theory and a principle of fairness. **Business Ethics Quarterly**, 7(01), pp. 51-66.

Puxty, A.G (1991). Social accountability and universal pragmatics, JAI Press.

Raffouriner B. (1995). The Determinants of Voluntary Financial Disclosure By Swiss Listed Companies. **European Accounting Review**, 4 (2), pp. 261-80.

Rahaman, A. S., Lawrence, S., and Roper, J. (2004). Social and environmental reporting at the VRA: institutionalized legitimacy or legitimation crisis? **Critical Perspectives on Accounting**, 15, pp. 35-56.

Ratanajongkol, S., Davey, H. and Low, M. (2006). Corporate social reporting in Thailand: the news is all good and increasing. **Qualitative Research in Accounting and Management** 3 (1) pp. 67-83.

Ratanajongkol, S., Davey, H., and Low, M. (2006) Corporate social reporting in Thailand: The news is all good and increasing. **Qualitative Research in Accounting & Management,** 3(1), pp. 67-83.

Rayman-Bacchus, L. (2006). Reflecting on corporate legitimacy. **Critical Perspectives on Accounting,** 17(2), pp. 323-335.

Rechner, P. L. and Dalton D.R (1989). The Impact of CEO as Board Chairperson on Corporate Performance: Evidence vs. Rhetoric, **Academy of Management Executive** Vol 3

Rechner, P.L. and D.R. Dalton, (1991). CEO duality and organizational perforMance: a longitudinal analysis. **Strategic Management Journal,** 12, (2), pp.155–160.

Reverte, C (2009) Determinants of Corporate Social Responsibility Disclosure Ratings by Spanish Listed Firms, **Journal of Business Ethics,** 88 (2), pp 351–366.

Reynolds, M., and Yuthas, K. (2008). Moral discourse and corporate social responsibility reporting. **Journal of Business Ethics,** 78(1-2), pp. 47-64.

Riahi-Belkaoui, A. (2001). The Role for Corporate Reputation for Multinational Firms: **Accounting, Organizational, and Market Considerations.** Westport, CT: Quorum.

Richardson, H. S. (1997) **Democratic intentions. The Modern Schoolman,** 74(4), 285-300.

Roberts R. W. (1992). Determinants of Corporate Social Responsibility Disclosure: an Application of Stakeholder Theory. **Accounting, Organization and Society,** 17 (6), pp. 595- 612.

Roberts, C. B. (1991). Environmental disclosures: a note on reporting practices in mainland Europe. **Accounting, Auditing and Accountability Journal,** 4 (3), pp. 62-71.

Roberts, R. W. (1992) Determinants of Corporate Social Responsibility Disclosure: An Application of Stakeholder Theory. **Accounting, Organizations and Society,** 17 (6) August, pp. 595–612.

Robertson, D.C. and N. Nicholson (1996). Expressions of Corporate Social Responsibility Quoted in Robson, C. (2002) **Real world research: A resource for social scientists and practitioner-researchers.** 2nd ed. Oxford: Blackwell.

Roca, L. C. and C. Searcy (2012). An analysis of indicators disclosed in corporate sustainability reports. **Journal of Cleaner Production,** 20 pp. 103-118.

Salzmann, O., Ionescu-Somers, A. and Steger, U. (2005). The business case for sustainability: literature review and research options. **European Management Journal,** 23 (1) pp. 27-36.

Schipper, K. (1991). Analysts' forecasts. **Accounting Horizons**, 5(4), pp. 105-121.

Seuring, S. and Muller, M. (2008). From a literature review to a conceptual framework for sustainable supply chain management. **Journal of Cleaner Production**,16 (15) pp. 1699-1710.

Shocker, A.D, and Sethi, S.P (1973). An approach to incorporating societal preferences in developing corporate action strategies, California: University of California Press

Silva Monteiro, S.M. and Aibar- Guzman, B (2010). "Determinants of environmental disclosure in the annual reports of large companies operating in Portugal", Corporate Social Responsibility And Environmental Management, Vol 17, Pages 185–204

Singh, D. R., and Ahuja, J. M. (1983). Corporate social reporting in India. **International Journal of Accounting,** 18(2), pp. 151-169.

Singhvi S. and Desai, H. (1971). An Empirical Analysis of the Quality of Corporate Financial Disclosure. **The Accounting Review,** 46 pp. 129-138.

Skouloudis, A. and Evangelinos, K.I. (2009). Sustainability reporting in Greece: are we there yet? **Environmental Quality Management,** 19 (1) pp. 43-59.

Skouloudis, A., Evangelinos, K. and Kourmousis, F. (2010) Assessing non-financial reports according to the Global Reporting Initiative guidelines: evidence from Greece. **Journal of Cleaner Production**, 18 pp. 426–438.

Slater, A. (2008) KPMG International Survey of Corporate Responsibility Reporting 2008. KPMG Global Sustainability Services, The Netherlands.

Smith C. W. Jr. and Watts, R.L. (1982). Incentive and tax effects of U.S. executive compensation plans. **Australian Journal of Management**, 7, pp. 139–157.

Smith Jr. C.W and Watts R.L (1986). The investment opportunity set and corporate financing, dividend, and compensation policies. **The Journal of Financial Economics**, 34. pp. 263-292.

Sobhani, F.A., Amran, A. and Zainuddin, Y. (2009). Revisiting the practices of corporate social and environmental disclosure in Bangladesh. **Corporate Social Responsibility and Environmental Management,** 16, pp. 167-183.

Solomon, R. and Hanson, K. (1985). **It's Good Business Atheneum,** New York (1985)

SRC Consult (2010). Development of CSR Guidelines for Mining Companies. Minerals Commission of Ghana.

Stanny, E., and Ely, K. (2008). Corporate environmental disclosures about the effects of climate change. **Corporate Social Responsibility and Environmental Management,** 15(6), pp. 338-348.

Stanton, P., and Stanton, J. (2002). Corporate annual reports: research perspectives used. **Accounting, Auditing & Accountability Journal,** 15(4), pp. 478-500.

Stanton-Salazar, R. (1997) A Social Capital Framework for Understanding the Socialization of Racial Minority Children and Youths. **Harvard Educational Review,** 67 (1), pp. 1-41.

Steurer, R. (2005). Mapping stakeholder theory anew: from the 'stakeholder theory of the firm'to three perspectives on business–society relations. **Business Strategy and the Environment,** 15(1), pp. 55-69.

Steurer, R. (2006). Mapping stakeholder theory anew: from the 'stakeholder theory of the firm' to three perspectives on business–society relations, **Business Strategy and the Environment.** 15, pp. 55–69.

Steurer, R., Langer, M. E., Konrad, A., and Martinuzzi, A., (2005). Corporations, stakeholders and sustainable development I: a theoretical exploration of businesse society relations. **Journal of Business Ethics,** 61, pp. 263-281.

Stewart J. D. (1984). The role of information in public accountability in Issues in Public Sector Accounting, Hopwood A. And C. Tomkins (eds) Oxford: Philip Allen. Stock Exchange Yearbook 1994-1995, The Macmillan.

Stiller, Y. and Daub, C. H. (2007). Paving the way for sustainable communication: evidence from a Swiss study. **Business Strategy and the Environment,** 16 pp. 474-486.

Stratos, (2008). Canadian Corporate Sustainability Reporting: Best Practices 2008. Stratos, Toronto.

Sturdivant and Ginter, S. (1977). Corporate Social Responsiveness. **California Management Review,** pp. 30–39.

Suchman, M.C. (1995). Managing legitimacy: strategic and institutional approaches. **Academy of Management Review,** 20 (3) pp. 571-610.

Thompson, P., & Zakaria, Z. (2004). Corporate Social Responsibility Reporting in Malaysia: Progress and Prospects. **The Journal of Corporate Citizenship,** (13), 125-136

Tilling, M.V., and Tilt C.A. (2010). The edge of legitimacy: Voluntary social and environmental reporting in Rothmans' 1956-1999 annual reports", **Accounting, Auditing & Accountability Journal,** 23(1), pp.55-81.

Tilt, C. A. (2001). The content and disclosure of Australian corporate environmental policies. **Accounting, Auditing & Accountability Journal,** 14 (2), pp.190 – 212.

Tilt, C. A., and Symes, C. F. (1999) Environmental disclosure by Australian mining companies: environmental conscience or commercial reality? **Accounting Forum**, 23 (2), pp. 137-154.

Tilt, C.A. (1994) The Influence of External Pressure Groups on Corporate Social Disclosure. Some Empirical Evidence. **Accounting, Auditing and Accountability Journal**, 7 (4) pp. 47–72.

Tricker, R. I. (1983). Corporate responsibility, institutional governance and the roles of accounting standards. **Accounting Standard Setting-an International Perspective. London**: Pitman.

Trierweiller, A. C., Peixe, B. C. S., Tezza, R., Bornia, A. C., and Campos L. M. S. (2012). Measuring environmental management disclosure in industries in Brazil with item response theory. **Journal of Cleaner Production**, 47, pp. 298-305.

Trotman, K. T., and Bradley, G. W. (1981). Associations between social responsibility disclosure and characteristics of companies. **Accounting, Organizations and Society**, 6 (4), pp. 355-362.

Uadiale and Fagbemi, (2012) Corporate Social Responsibility and Financial Performance in Developing Economies: The Nigerian Experience. **Journal of Economics and Sustainable Development**, 3 (4).

Ullmann, A. A. (1985). Data in search of a theory: a critical examination of the relationships among social performance, social disclosure, and economic performance of U. S. firms. **The Academy of Management Review**, 10 (3), pp. 540-557.

UNCTAD, T. (1996). Development report 1996. United Nations, Geneva.

Unerman, J. (2000) Methodological issues - Reflections on quantification in corporate social reporting content analysis. **Accounting, Auditing & Accountability Journal**, 13 (5), pp.667 – 681.

Utaminingtyas, T. H. and Ahalik. (2010). The Relationship Between Corporate Social Responsibility and Earnings Response Coefficient: Evidence from Indonesian Stock Exchange. Oxford Business & Economic Program.

Van Berkel R., and Bossilkov, A (2004). Sustainable development reporting in the Australian minerals processing industry, Green processing Conference

Van Marrewijk, M. (2003). Concepts and definitions of CSR and corporate sustainability: Between agency and communion. **Journal of business ethics**, 44(2-3), pp.95-105.

van Staden, and Hooks, J. (2007) A comprehensive comparison of corporate environmental reporting and responsiveness. **British Accounting Review.** 39 (3) (2007), pp. 197–210.

VanMarrewijk, M. (2003) Concepts and definitions of CSR and corporate sustainability: between agency and communion. **Journal of Business Ethics,** 44 (2) pp. 95-105.

Veleva, V. and Ellenbecker, M. (2001) Indicators of sustainable production: framework and methodology. **Journal of Cleaner Production** 9 pp. 519-549.

Verrecchia, R.E (1983) "Discretionary disclosure", **Journal of Accounting and Economics,** Vol 5

Vormedal, I., and Ruud, A. (2009). Sustainability reporting in Norway–an assessment of performance in the context of legal demands and socio-political drivers. **Business Strategy and the Environment,** 18(4), pp. 207-222.

Waddock, S.A., and S.B. Graves. (1994). Industry Performance and Investment in R&D and Capital Goods. **The Journal of High Technology Management Research,** 5 (1), pp. 1-17.

Wallace, R.S.O. & Naser, K (1995) Firm-specific determinants of the comprehensiveness of mandatory disclosure in the corporate annual reports of firms listed on the stock exchange of Hong Kong, **Journal of Accounting and Public Policy,** Vol 14

Wang, K., Sewon, O. and Claiborne, M. C. (2008). Determinants and consequences of voluntary disclosure in an emerging market: Evidence from China. **Journal of International Accounting, Auditing and Taxation,** 17 (1) pp. 14–30.

Watson, A., Shrives, P., and Marston, C. (2002). Voluntary disclosure of accounting ratios in the UK. **British Accounting Review.** 34, (4), pp. 289-313

Watts R. L., Zimmerman J. L, (1986). Positivr Accounting Theory, Prentice-Hall Inc.

Watts, R. L. and Zimmerman, J.L. (1990). Positive accounting theory: A ten year perspective. **The Accounting Review,** 65 (1), pp. 131–156.

Weber, R. (1990). **Quantitative applications in the social sciences: Basic content analysis.** 2nd ed. Beverly Hills, Calif: Sage Publications.

Weber, R. P. (1990). **Basic Content Analysis, Sage University Paper Series on Quantitative Applications in the Social Sciences,** Series No. 49 2nd ed. Newbury Park: Sage Publications.

White, H. (1980). A heteroskedasticity-consistent covariance matrix and a direct test for heteroskedasticity. **Econometrica,** 48, pp. 817-838.

Williamson O.E (1970). **Corporate control and business behavior: An inquiry into the effects of organization form on enterprise behavior,** Prentice Hall

Williamson, O. (1963). Managerial Discretion and Business Behavior. **The American Economic Review,** 53(5), 1032-1057.

Willis, A. (2003). The role of the global reporting initiative's sustainability reporting guidelines in the social screening of investments. **Journal of Business Ethics,** 43 (3), pp. 233-7.

Wilmshurst, T. D. and Frost, G. R. (2000). Corporate environmental reporting: A test of legitimacy theory. **Accounting, Auditing & Accountability Journal,** 13 (1), pp.10 – 26.

Wiseman, J. (1982). An evaluation of environmental disclosures made in corporate annual reports. **Accounting, Organizations and Society,** 7 (1), pp. 53-63.

Wood, D. J. (1991). Corporate Social Performance Revisited, **The Academy of Management Review** Vol. 16, No. 4 (Oct., 1991)

Woodward, D. G., Edwards, P. and Birkin, F. (1996), Organizational Legitimacy and Stakeholder Information Provision1. British Journal of Management, 7

Woodward, D., Edwards, P. and Birkin, F. (2001). Some evidence on executives' views of corporate social responsibility. **British Accounting Review.** 33 (3), pp. 357-397.

World Commission on Environment and Development (WCED), (1987). **Our Common Future.** Oxford University Press, Oxford, UK.

Xiao J.Z., Gao, S. S., Heravi, S., Chueng, Y.C.K., (2005). "The Impact of Social and Economic Development on Corporate Social and Environmental Disclosure in Hong Kong and the U.K.", **Advances in International Accounting,** 18, pp. 219-243.

Yin, R.K. (2009). **In: Case Study Research: Design and Methods.** 4th ed. SAGE Publications, Thousand Oaks, California, USA.

Zadek, S (2007). Global collaborative governance: there is no alternative, Corporate Governance: The international journal of business in society, 8, pp.374-388.

Zadek, S, Raynard, P, Forstater, M, and Oelschlaegel, J (2004). The future of sustainability assurance, ACCA Research Report.

Zarzeski M. T. (1996). Spontaneous harmonization effects of culture and market forces on accounting disclosure practices. **Accounting Horizons** 10(1), pp. 18–37.

Zeghal S. D. and Ahmed, A. (1990) Comparison of Social Responsibility Information Disclosure Media Used by Canadian Firms. **Accounting, Auditing & Accountability Journal,** 3 (1) pp. 38 49.

Ziegler, A. and Schröder, M. (2010). What determines the inclusion in a sustainability stock index? A panel data analysis for European firms. **Ecological Economics,** 69, pp. 848-856.

www.ingramcontent.com/pod-product-compliance
Lightning Source LLC
Chambersburg PA
CBHW030758180526
45163CB00003B/1075